3rd Edition

Elementary

MARKET LEADER

Business English Practice File

John Rogers

	LANGUAGE WORK			TALK BUSINESS	
	VOCABULARY	**LANGUAGE REVIEW**	**WRITING**	**SOUND WORK**	**SURVIVAL BUSINESS ENGLISH**
UNIT 1 INTRODUCTIONS page 4 /page 54	Review and extension: Countries and nationalities	*to be*	Editing E-mails	**Individual sounds:** Countries and nationalities **Connected speech:** Linking words together **Stress and intonation:** Stressed syllables	Introducing yourself and others Listening practice
UNIT 2 WORK AND LEISURE page 8 /page 56	Work and leisure activities Days, months, dates Review and extension: Prepositions	Present simple Adverbs and expressions of frequency	Spelling Capital letters Forms E-mails	**Individual sounds:** /ɪ/ and /aɪ/ Third person -*s* **Connected speech:** Linking words together	Questions and answers Listening practice
UNIT 3 PROBLEMS page 12 /page 58	Problems at work *too/enough/very*	Present simple: negatives and questions *Have; some* and *any*	Spelling Punctuation Linkers: *and/but* Letters	**Individual sounds:** The letter *a* **Connected speech:** *Do you?* **Stress and intonation:** Stressing important words	What's the problem? Listening practice
UNIT 4 TRAVEL page 16 /page 60	Travel Collocations Review and extension: Prepositions	*can/can't* *there is/there are* Extension: *there* and *it*	Editing Hotel bookings	**Individual sounds:** The letter *o* **Connected speech:** *can/can't* **Stress and intonation:** Polite requests	Using stress to correct information Listening practice
UNIT 5 FOOD AND ENTERTAINING page 20 /page 62	Review and extension: Eating out Review and extension: Collocations	Countable and uncountable nouns *much, many a lot of*	Editing Messages E-mails	**Individual sounds:** /ɪ/ and /iː/ **Connected speech:** Weak forms: *for, some, of* **Stress and intonation:** Word stress	Eating out Listening practice
UNIT 6 BUYING AND SELLING page 24 /page 64	Review and extension: Buying and selling Extension: Collocations	Past simple	Editing Letters	**Individual sounds:** Matching sounds Forms of *to be* **Stress and intonation:** Regular past forms	Sales talk Listening practice

THE SOUNDS OF ENGLISH: page 52	**USING A DICTIONARY:** page 53	**SOUNDS AND SPELLING:** page 53

	LANGUAGE WORK			TALK BUSINESS	
	VOCABULARY	LANGUAGE REVIEW	WRITING	SOUND WORK	SURVIVAL BUSINESS ENGLISH
UNIT 7 PEOPLE *page 28 /page 66*	Adjectives to describe people Prepositions	Past simple: negatives and questions Question forms	Linkers: *because/but/so* Editing	Groups of consonants **Connected speech:** Linking words together **Stress and intonation:** *Wh-* questions	Management issues Listening practice
UNIT 8 ADVERTISING *page 32/page 68*	Advertising and markets	Comparatives and superlatives Extension: *much/a lot, a little/a bit*	E-mails	**Individual sounds:** The *schwa* sound: /ə/ **Connected speech:** Comparative forms **Stress and intonation:** Word stress	Meetings Listening practice
UNIT 9 COMPANIES *page 36 /page 70*	Companies	Present continuous Present simple or present continuous?	Editing Company literature	Silent letters **Connected speech:** *are, aren't, isn't*	Talks and presentations Listening practice
UNIT 10 COMMUNICATION *page 40 /page 72*	Internal communication Prepositions	Future forms	Word order E-mails	**Individual sounds:** /v/ and /w/ **Connected speech:** Future forms **Stress and intonation:** Using stress to correct information	Making arrangements Listening practice
UNIT 11 CULTURES *page 44 /page 74*	Company cultures	*should/ shouldn't* *could/would*	Linkers: *and/because/ but/so* Topic sentences	Groups of consonants **Connected speech:** *should* and *shouldn't* **Stress and intonation:** *Schwa* in unstressed syllables Sounding polite	Conversations Listening practice
UNIT 12 JOBS *page 48 /page 76*	Skills and abilities Prepositions	Present perfect Past simple or present perfect?	Word order Job applications	*-ed* endings **Individual sounds:** /ɒ/ and /ɔː/ **Connected speech:** Contractions	A job interview Listening practice

Introductions

VOCABULARY

A **Write the letters in the correct order to make the names of countries.**

1 Cainh   *China* ....

2 Risasu   ....

3 Sendew   ....

4 Planod   ....

5 Gyranem   ....

6 Aganirten   ....

B **Write the missing letters to make nationalities.**

1 Fadilah is O̲ m a̲ n i̲ .

2 Mr Nakamura is J _ p _ n _ _ _ .

3 Christophe Boulan is F _ _ n _ h.

4 Ms Isabel Caceres is S _ _ n i _ h.

5 Andrew Harrison is E _ _ l _ _ h.

6 Vassiliki is G _ _ e _ .

C **Use the clues to complete the crossword puzzle.**

Across

1 Philip Clarke is the CEO of Tesco, the largest *British* .... supermarket chain. (7)

6 Ingvar Kamprad, founder of Ikea, is from .... (6)

8 .... companies like Microsoft and GE are among the world's most respected companies. (2)

9 Toyota and Nissan are two carmakers from .... (5)

11 Lee Kun-hee is Chairman of Samsung, the famous .... technology company. (6)

Down

1 Natura, Petrobras and Weg are three companies from .... (6)

2 Lakshmi Mittal is from .... He is Chief Executive of Arcelor Mittal, the world's biggest steelmaker. (5)

3 Nestlé is one of the most famous .... companies. (5)

4 Nokia, a .... company, makes high-quality mobile phones. (7)

5 BMW, Porsche and Volkswagen are three carmakers from .... (7)

7 Jean-Paul Agon, L'Oréal's Chief Executive, is from .... (6)

10 British Airways, Virgin Atlantic and easyJet are airlines from the .... (2)

VOCABULARY +

D **Here are six adjectives. Write the names of the corresponding countries.**

1 Danish .....*Denmark*.....
2 Dutch ....
3 Pakistani ....

4 Czech ....
5 Turkish ....
6 Senegalese ....

E **Here are six countries. Write the corresponding adjectives.**

1 Norway .....*Norwegian*.....
2 Portugal ....
3 Switzerland ....

4 Taiwan ....
5 Slovakia ....
6 Thailand ....

F **Complete the groups below with the names of countries from the box and their corresponding nationality adjectives.**

| Bahrain | Chile | Iran | Iraq | Finland | Scotland | Sudan | Vietnam |

Group 1
Adjectives ending in -an

Country	Nationality
Brazil	Brazil**ian**
Germany	Germa**n**
....	....
....	....

Group 2
Adjectives ending in -ish

Country	Nationality
Poland	Pol**ish**
Spain	Span**ish**
....	....
....	....

Group 3
Adjectives ending in -ese

Country	Nationality
Japan	Japan**ese**
China	Chin**ese**
....	....
....	....

Group 4
Adjectives ending in -i

Country	Nationality
Kuwait	Kuwait**i**
Oman	Oman**i**
....	....
....	....

LANGUAGE REVIEW

to be

A **Complete the sentences with words from the box. In some places both the full form and the contracted form are possible.**

| am | 'm | are | 're | is | 's |

1 Lucien and Marie-Claire .....*are*........ our agents in Bordeaux.
2 Mrs Turner .... a programmer in Leeds.
3 My boss and I .... from Frankfurt.
4 Where .... your new assistant from?
5 Excuse me, ... you the new technician?
6 I .... Swiss, but my company .... Italian.
7 Dorota and Cezariusz .... Polish. Their office .... in Poznan.

B **Rewrite the sentences with the correct form(s) of the verb *to be* in the correct place(s).**

1 His English very good.
His English is very good.

2 Where they from?
....

3 What her name?
....

4 My office in Paris, but I not French.
....

5 Mrs Lopez a lawyer.
....

6 Alex and Rob from Italy.
....

C **Write the words in the correct order to make questions. You need one word from the box for each question.**

am are is

1 your / Ingrid / name / ?
Is your name Ingrid?

2 Spain / Isabel and Luis / from / ?
....

3 a / you / programmer / ?
....

4 Marketing / in / you and Tom / ?
....

5 I / tomorrow / in / room 16 / ?
....

D **Match the sentence halves.**

1 I'm in Sales,

2 She's in Accounts,

3 My assistant and I are in a meeting all day

4 You aren't in the city centre,

5 It's only 9.50

a) but she isn't an accountant.

b) so we aren't free.

c) so you aren't late.

d) but you are very near the conference hall.

e) but I'm not a sales representative.

E **Write short answers to the questions.**

1 Is Ákos from Turkey?
No, he isn't. He's from Hungary.

2 Are you in Production too, Maria?
.... I'm the assistant production manager.

3 Am I in room 243 tomorrow?
.... You're in room 112.

4 Am I late for the meeting?
.... But just by five minutes so don't worry.

5 Is Linda English, too?
.... She's from Australia.

6 Is the new sales assistant French?
.... He's from Lyons.

7 Are you from Switzerland, Brigitte?
.... I'm from Belgium.

8 Are you and Lucille in Marketing?
.... We're both in Finance.

WRITING

Editing

A **Rewrite the sentences with the words from the box in the correct places.**

| a̶ are do from is (x3) |

1 Is your wife manager?
  Is your wife a manager?

2 She married with two children.
  ....

3 Lucas and Mirjana interested in travel.
  ....

4 Wizz Air a Hungarian company?
  ....

5 How you do? I'm Ana Kostic, from RTVS.
  ....

6 The sales manager very busy today.
  ....

7 My best friend is Brazilian. He is Porto Seguro.
  ....

B **Put apostrophes (') where necessary.**

1 Her name's Paola.

2 Akemis from Japan.

3 Her companys in Osaka.

4 Whats your job?

5 Its very modern, but it isnt very large.

6 'Are you and your colleague from Poland?' – 'No, we arent. Were from Ukraine.'

C **Rewrite the sentences with capital letters where necessary.**

1 nikola iș from croatia.
  Nikola iș from Croatia.

2 mrs kimura is japanese.
  ....

3 is nokia danish?
  ....

4 paul is married with two children.
  ....

5 this is george ellis, from marketing.
  ....

6 mr brown's new boss is from london, ontario.
  ....

E-mails

D **You are at an international trade fair in another country. You write an e-mail about the fair to a colleague in your office. Complete the e-mail with items from the box.**

| a sales manager   business is   company sells
| do business   is a great city   is from Altheim |

> **To:** RTodorovic@easynet.co.uk
> **From:** Max.Lang@lycos.com
> **Subject:** Cyberfair
>
> Hi!
> The Cyberfair is very exciting, and Frankfurt *is a great city*[1]. There are interesting people from all over the world here at the fair. Andreas Wallner.
> ....[2] in Austria. He's ....[3].
> His ....[4] furniture for hi-tech offices and he says ....[5] good at the moment. I think Mr Wallner is a very good business contact. I'm sure we can ....[6] with him.
>
> Bye for now,
> Max

Work and leisure

VOCABULARY

A **Complete the sentences.**

1 Tom says friendly colleagues are more important than a h _igh_ s_alary_.
2 I can start work at 7.30, 8.30 or 9.30. I'm really glad I can work f _ _ _ _ _ _ _ h _ _ _ _.
3 Her job has a lot of t _ _ _ _ _ o _ _ _ _ _ _ _ _ _ _ _. She goes to a different country every month!
4 When I travel on business, the company pays for my meals and my hotels. It's so easy when you have an e _ _ _ _ _ _ a _ _ _ _ _ _.
5 My company has a gym, a swimming pool and many other s _ _ _ _ _ f _ _ _ _ _ _ _ _ _.
6 All our sales representatives use c _ _ _ _ _ _ c _ _ _ to visit customers in other cities.
7 I drive to work so I'm glad my company has free p _ _ _ _ _ _ f _ _ _ _ _ _ _ _ _.
8 For me, j _ _ s _ _ _ _ _ _ _ is what I need most. I have three children so I don't want to be out of work.

B **Write the missing letters to make names of days, months or seasons.**

1 Th_ursday_
2 _ _ _ _ h
3 _ i _ _ _ _
4 _ _ b _ _ _ _ _
5 _ _ _ _ d _ _
6 _ _ t _ _ _

C **Complete the sentences with *at, in* or *on*.**

1 Our departmental meeting is ..._on_... Friday afternoon.
2 I don't like meetings .... the morning.
3 The first interview is .... 17th December.
4 The second interview is .... January.
5 When he travels all day, he can't sleep .... night.
6 She usually visits our head office .... the autumn.
7 They never work .... the weekend.
8 Are you free .... Wednesday?
9 Susan sometimes works .... Saturdays.
10 Do you often go out .... the evening?
11 He starts his first meeting .... 8.30.

D **Write Ʌ to show the place of the missing word in each sentence. Write the word on the line.**

1 Some of my colleagues love listening Ʌ hard rock. ...._to_........
2 My boss and I don't like watching football TV. ....
3 My colleagues and I often go to cinema on Saturdays. ....
4 I quite like reading, but I hate to the radio. ....
5 Our new secretary sometimes tennis at the weekend. ....
6 How often do you go abroad holiday? ....

VOCABULARY + **E** **Complete the time phrases in the sentences with *at* or *in*. Write Ø if no word is missing.**

1 Can I see you ...Ø... next Tuesday?
2 They'll deliver the goods ...... the end of the month.
3 We need to have a meeting ...... this afternoon.
4 The office closes ...... 6.00 p.m.
5 There's a staff party ...... every December.
6 Our visitors arrive ...... three hours' time.
7 She worked very hard ...... last winter.
8 Hurry up! The bank closes ...... ten minutes.
9 He travelled to China ...... 1999.
10 I'm sorry. Mrs Moor's in a meeting ...... the moment.

> **What's the rule?**
>
> Study the sentences above and complete the rule.
>
> We do **not** use *at*, *in* or *on* before *next*, ..., ... or .... in a time phrase.

F **In each box, match the words that go together to find more things to do in your free time. Use a good dictionary to help you.**

1 stay in	a) to concerts
2 play	b) a novel
3 read	c) a party
4 go	d) with your family
5 have	e) computer games

6 listen	a) jogging
7 go for	b) DVDs
8 go	c) a walk
9 work in	d) to music on my iPod
10 watch	e) the garden

LANGUAGE REVIEW

Present simple

A **Complete the information about Kati Varga with the correct form of verbs from the box.**

| arrive | check | enjoy | ~~get~~ | go | have | have | like | spend | work |

Kati Varga's working day

Kati Varga is the director of Commerzbank, a large bank in Budapest. She *gets* ....[1] up at about 5.30 and usually goes jogging in the park. Then she ....[2] a shower and prepares breakfast for herself and her family. 'We all ....[3] to have breakfast together,' she says, 'and that's great.'

She ....[4] to work by metro. She ....[5] at her office between 7.45 and 8 o'clock. Then she works at her desk for half an hour. 'I always ....[6] my e-mail first thing every morning,' she says.

At 8.30 she starts her first meeting. She ....[7] a lot of meetings in the morning with customers and also with other important bankers. 'I keep the afternoons free for staff meetings,' she says.

Two or three nights a week Ms Varga ....[8] late at the office. She gets home late and often goes to bed after midnight.

She travels a lot and ....[9] about 50 days abroad every year. In her free time, she likes hiking and playing tennis. 'And when the weather is nice, my family and I really ....[10] sailing,' she says.

LANGUAGE WORK

LANGUAGE WORK

Adverbs and expressions of frequency

B **Rewrite the sentences with the words in brackets in the correct place.**

1 Tina has lunch in the company cafeteria. (never)
   Tina never has lunch in the company cafeteria.

2 Jameel goes to conferences abroad. (sometimes)
   ....

3 Rick isn't very busy on Mondays. (usually)
   ....

4 We are at home in the evening. (never)
   ....

5 Do you go to work by train? (always)
   ....

6 James does not travel on business. (often)
   ....

7 I stay at home at the weekend. (usually)
   ....

8 Why are some people late for work? (always)
   ....

C **Write the words in the correct order to make sentences.**

1 I / have / with / lunch / often / colleagues.
   I often have lunch with colleagues.

2 How / Sedef / often / does / visit / clients?

3 Darius / a / twice / late / works / week.

4 In / evening, / watch / the / we / usually / TV.

5 They / at / are / home / on / never / Saturdays.

6 She / a lot of / calls / every / makes / telephone / day.

WRITING
Spelling

A **Complete the verbs.**

1 Lucy go.*es*. to work by bus.

2 She arri.... at work at 8.45 a.m.

3 She star.... work at 9 o'clock.

4 In the morning, she discu.... new plans with her colleagues.

5 She often h.... lunch in the staff cafeteria.

6 She enj.... her job a lot.

7 In the evening, she stu.... for her MBA.

Capital letters

B **Rewrite the sentences with capital letters where necessary.**

1 vera works till 5.30 on thursdays.
   Vera works till 5.30 on Thursdays.

2 she goes to the uk every year in march.
   ....

3 paul sometimes reads *the financial times*.
   ....

4 they live in amsterdam, but they aren't dutch.
   ....

5 their office is in oxford street.
   ....

6 as you know, i work for the european commission.

....

7 the polish representatives arrive at heathrow at 7.30 a.m.

....

8 louise and bill are from the united states.

....

9 how often do you watch the bbc?

....

Forms **C** **Read the text and complete the form.**

Hello! My name's Raoul Gautier and I'm the PR* Manager with the Banque de l'Ouest. It's a new job for me and I like it very much.

My address is 47, Avenue Aristide Briand, Toulouse and my phone number is +33 555 78 43 00.

I'm 24 years old – the same age as my partner, Sarah. We're getting married next year!

First name:	....
Surname:	....
Age:	....
Marital status:	Single/Married
Occupation:	....
Address:	....
	....
Telephone number:	....

*PR is short for Public Relations.

E-mails **D** **Raoul Gautier is the new PR Manager with the Banque de l'Ouest in Toulouse. Number the sentences of his e-mail to the staff in the correct order.**

From:	RGautier@banqueouest.fr
To:	staff@banqueouest.fr
Subject:	New PR Manager

Dear All,

a) I also have to give them information about our work. ☐

b) This is just to introduce myself. [1]

c) I look forward to meeting you all at our staff meeting on Friday. ☐

d) My main responsibility is to communicate with the public and the media. ☐

e) My name is Raoul Gautier and I am the new PR Manager. ☐

With best wishes,
Raoul Gautier

Problems

LANGUAGE WORK

VOCABULARY

A **Complete the sentences.**

1 Let's take a taxi. We don't want to be l _a_ _t_ _e_ for the meeting.
2 The documents aren't in the envelope. They're m _ _ _ _ _ _ .
3 It's a new computer, but it c _ _ _ _ _ _ two or three times a week.
4 Don't sit on that chair! It's b _ _ _ _ _ _ .
5 Oh no! The photocopier is not w _ _ _ _ _ _.

B **Match the sentences (1–7) with the sentences (a–g).**

1 I think Alpha Tours is too expensive.
2 It's too far to walk.
3 The office is really too small.
4 The interviewer talks too fast.
5 There isn't enough information in this report.
6 They say the Royal Hotel isn't good enough.
7 This machine's too slow.

a) We need more detail.
b) Please book my flight with a different company.
c) It takes three minutes to make ten copies.
d) Let's take a taxi.
e) It's difficult to understand her.
f) There isn't enough space for all the staff.
g) They want to stay at the Astoria.

C **Correct the sentences that are wrong.**

1 I can afford to buy the LJ200 printer, but it's ~~too~~ expensive.   _very_
2 This mobile phone is too big to fit in my pocket.
3 It's too late to telephone. They close at 5.30.
4 My boss is great and my colleagues are too nice.
5 I can't do it enough fast. I need some help.
6 Come to our country! The food is delicious and the people are too friendly.

D **Match the adjectives with their opposites.**

1 unpleasant
2 relaxing
3 noisy
4 negative
5 expensive

a) stressful
b) cheap
c) positive
d) pleasant
e) quiet

6 efficient
7 dirty
8 boring
9 clear
10 difficult

f) interesting
g) inefficient
h) confusing
i) easy
j) clean

E **Choose the best word (a, b or c) to complete each sentence.**

1 You always say business is not very good. Come on, try to be a bit more .._positive_..
   a) positive
   b) negative
   c) boring

2 I don't like my new office chair. It's not .... enough.
   a) narrow
   b) rude
   c) wide

3 Yasmina always does a lot of work and she works so fast! She's very .... , isn't she?
   a) modern
   b) positive
   c) efficient

4   The trade show was really exciting, but the speech at the beginning was
    quite ....
    a) boring   b) cheap   c) interesting
5   Jeff doesn't like his new job. He says it's stressful and .... paid.
    a) well   b) badly   c) rude
6   Tickets for the concert are too .... Let's take our visitors to a
    restaurant instead.
    a) easy   b) expensive   c) difficult
7   Can you help, please? These instructions are very .... !
    a) unpleasant   b) clear   c) confusing

LANGUAGE REVIEW

Present simple: negatives and questions

A **Write the opposite of these sentences.**

1   They report to the director.   *They don't report to the director.*
2   She doesn't start very early.   *She starts very early.*
3   She finishes work late.   ....
4   We don't often work at the weekend. ....
5   They sell office equipment.   ....
6   I make a lot of phone calls.   ....
7   He doesn't write reports.   ....

B **Study the information in the table. Then complete the sentences.**

		Kate and Ross	Jim
1	Do you often travel abroad?	✗	✓
2	Do you get lots of e-mails?	✓	✗
3	Do you have regular breaks?	✗	✓
4	Do you attend a lot of meetings?	✓	✗
5	Do you often entertain foreign visitors?	✗	✓
6	Do you read *The Financial Times*?	✓	✗

1   Kate and Ross *don't often travel abroad*
2   Jim .... e-mails.
3   Jim .... breaks.
4   Kate and Ross .... meetings.
5   Kate and Ross .... visitors.
6   Jim .... *The Financial Times*.

C **Study the information in exercise B again. Then complete the sentences, as in the example.**

*Kate and Ross don't often travel abroad, but **Jim does**.*

NOT (**Kate and Ross don't often travel abroad, but Jim often travels abroad.*)

1   Kate and Ross .... lots of e-mails, but ....
2   Kate and Ross .... regular breaks, but ....
3   Jim .... a lot of meetings, but ....
4   Jim often .... visitors, but ....
5   .... *The Financial Times*, but .... doesn't.

Have*; *some* and *any

D **Complete the sentences with *a*, *some* or *any*.**

1 We've .*some*. problems with cash flow this month.

2 Joe's office has air conditioning, but it doesn't have .... windows.

3 The invoice is incorrect. Please send us .... new one.

4 My new office doesn't have .... very nice view.

5 Do you have .... meetings on Tuesday?

6 We don't have .... information about the missing documents.

7 Does he have .... problems with the new boss?

8 Please give us .... details.

9 They don't have .... Korean customers.

10 Ms Torres has .... meetings on Friday, but she's free on Monday.

WRITING

Spelling

A **Write the full forms.**

1 We'd like to inform you that there's a problem with the printer.
We would like to inform you that there is a problem with the printer.

2 Their company's having a problem with their cash flow.
....

3 Our order's delayed.
....

4 It doesn't work properly.
....

5 It's very efficient.
....

6 She doesn't have an assistant.
....

> **Tip**
> When you write a business letter or a report, always use the full forms.

Punctuation

B **Separate the words and punctuate the sentences. Use capital letters where necessary.**

1 healwayssendshisreportsontime
He always sends his reports on time.

2 theypayalotofrentforasmallofficeinthecitycentre

3 whendoesthemeetingfinish

4 billhasalargeoffice,buthedoesnothaveacompanycar

5 howmanypeopledotheyemploy

Linkers: *and/but*

C **Match the sentence halves. Then link them with *and* or *but*.**

1 He is a good team player
2 She is always on time
3 The new machine is small
4 The report is very long
5 There are a lot of changes
6 Our office is small

a) it is very heavy.
b) it is very easy to understand.
c) she is very efficient.
d) it is in the city centre.
e) he does not go to meetings.
f) staff are worried about their jobs.

1 *He is a good team player, but he does not go to meetings.*

Letters   **D**   **Complete the letter with words from the box.**

| damaged | inform | missing | ~~October~~ | problem | send |

SIMONS SECURITY SERVICES
Manor Road, Holdenby, Northampton, NN8 9TJ

David Ashby,
Crawley Electronics,
27 Old London Road,
Benson,
Oxon, OX10 3RL

15th _October_.[1]

Dear Mr Ashby
Subject: Our order Ref. PJ/66

We would like to ....[2] you that we have a ....[3] with the
printer you delivered this morning.
The box is ....[4] and there is a piece ....[5]. (Ref. no. ASD32/S).
In addition, there is no instruction manual.
Could you please ....[6] us the missing part and the manual as soon
as possible.

We look forward to hearing from you.

Yours sincerely
Jane Warren

Jane Warren

Product Manager

Note

The box is damaged. There is a piece missing. There is no instruction manual.
Notice how you can **link** this information.
The box is damaged **and** there is a piece missing. **In addition**, there is no
instruction manual.

E   **Make sentences using the linkers in the same way.**

1   The office is small. The office is crowded. The air conditioning does not work.
   ....

2   The screen is small. The picture is not very good. There is no remote control.
   ....

3   The photocopier does not work. There is only one phone line. The receptionist is
   never on time.
   ....

LANGUAGE WORK

VOCABULARY **A** Use the clues to complete the crossword puzzle.

Across

1 Can I take this as hand .....*luggage*....? (7)

5 Going through .... checks sometimes takes a long time. (8)

6 Travelling is OK, but I hate .... all those suitcases before the trip! (7)

9 Mr Komano .... at 16.45. I'll go and pick him up at the airport. (7)

12 All Paris trains .... from platform 8. (5)

Down

2 Passengers for flight BA247 to São Paulo, please go to 71. (4)

3 Do you have any ....-free goods? (4)

4 A .... ticket to the city centre, please. (6)

7 Could I have an .... call at 5.30 a.m. tomorrow, please? (5)

8 Please .... your seatbelts and switch off any electronic devices. (6)

10 You are in .... 12, seat B. (3)

11 Would you like an aisle or a window .... ? (4)

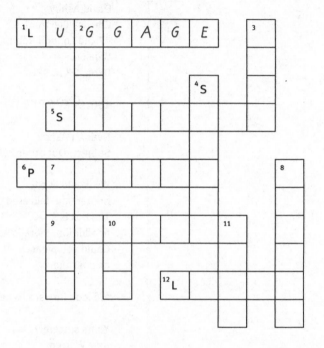

Collocations **B** Cross out the word that does not normally go with the word in the bubble.

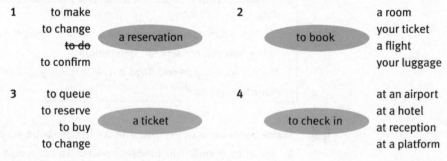

1
to make
to change
~~to do~~
to confirm

a reservation

2
a room
your ticket
a flight
your luggage

to book

3
to queue
to reserve
to buy
to change

a ticket

4
at an airport
at a hotel
at reception
at a platform

to check in

VOCABULARY +

C **Complete the sentences with words from the box.**

| at (x3) by (x2) for from (x2) off on to (x5) |

1 A lot of my colleagues go to work ..by.. car.
2 I go to the office .... foot. It takes me 35 minutes.
3 Sometimes, I go .... bus. That takes me about 20 minutes.
4 I get .... the bus at the City Park, then I walk .... the office.
5 I start work .... 9 o'clock, but I like to arrive .... the office early.
6 How long does it take to get .... here .... your office?
7 The plane arrives .... 2.20.
8 It's a great airport. You never wait very long .... your luggage.
9 Passengers for flight BA784 .... Rome, please go .... gate 36.
10 Could you book me a room .... 30th August .... 3rd September, please?

D **Match the verbs with their opposites. Use a good dictionary to help you.**

1 to land   a) to arrive
2 to leave   b) to be on time
3 to get off   c) to take off
4 to be delayed   d) to miss
5 to catch   e) to get on

E **Complete the sentences with the correct form of a verb from exercise D.**

1 There is sometimes a last security check just before the plane ..takes off..
2 Be polite and wait for people to .... the train before you ....
3 Don't .... the 8.30 Intercity! The next one isn't until 11 o'clock.
4 Right. So departure time is 4.25. What time does it .... ?
5 We regret to announce that all trains .... because of the snow.

LANGUAGE REVIEW

can/can't

A **Write the questions (1–9) in the correct column, according to the meaning of *can*.**

(ability)	(permission)	(what is possible)
2 Can you use the new photocopier?		1 Can we fly direct from Rome to Tashkent?

1 Can we fly direct from Rome to Tashkent?
2 Can you use the new photocopier?
3 Can she speak Russian?
4 Can I use your computer for half an hour, please?
5 Where can I buy phone cards?
6 Excuse me. Can I open the window?
7 Can you hear me now?
8 Can I just make a phone call, please?
9 Can we go to the airport by underground?

LANGUAGE WORK

B **Match the answers (a–i) with the questions (1–9) in exercise A.**

a) Yes. You don't need to change.

b) Yes, you can, but you need to change twice from here.

c) At the post office. A lot of kiosks sell them, too.

d) Sure! It's really hot in here.

e) Yes, go ahead. Just dial 9 to get an outside line.

f) Yes, of course. You can use it all morning if you like. I'll be in a meeting.

g) Yes, that's better. It's not a very good line, is it?

h) No, I can't. But I want to learn.

i) Yes. And her Chinese is quite good, too.

1
9

there is /
there are

C **Complete the sentences with the correct form of *there is* or *there are*.**

1 The area is a bit boring. ..*There isn't*.. anywhere to go after 7 o'clock in the evening.

2 What can we do? .... a very long queue at the ticket office.

3 .... any direct flights to Brussels on Tuesdays or Thursdays, I'm afraid.

4 I'm afraid .... a small problem with your reservation, sir.

5 It's great! .... lots of shops near our hotel.

6 .... a fitness centre at the Victoria Hotel?

7 Oh dear! .... any meeting rooms available next week.

8 .... Internet access in each room?

9 I think .... two direct flights a day.

10 It's an excellent hotel, but .... a swimming pool.

LANGUAGE +

there* and *it

D **Complete the sentences with *there* or *it*.**

1 ..*There*..'s another flight at 10.15. ..*It*..'s a Lufthansa flight.

2 'Is .... a gift shop?' 'Yes, madam. ....'s on the first floor.'

3 ....'s too late, ...'s nobody at the office.

4 I know the Astoria. ....'s an excellent hotel and ....'s very near the airport.

5 ....'s Internet access in each room and ....'s free.

6 Podgorica? I know ....'s the capital of Montenegro, but what kind of place is ....? Is .... anywhere to go in the evening?

WRITING

Editing

A **Rewrite the sentences with the words from the box in the correct places.**

are	confirm	~~double~~	from	like	station

1 Do you want a single or a room?
Do you want a single or a double room?

2 I'd like to book a room Sunday 5th to Thursday 9th of this month.
....

3 I'm ringing to my flight details.
....

4 Would you an aisle or a window seat?
....

5 Can we meet at the railway at 8.30?
....

6 There two restaurants where you can entertain business guests.
....

Hotel bookings

B **Complete the e-mail with words and phrases from the box.**

~~book~~   booking   costs   hotel   per night   please   thank   two nights

To: Lise.Belfort@aquarius.fr
From: Aquarius.Infotech@skynetcom.ca
Subject: Travel arrangements

Dear Lise,

As you know, our General Manager, Linda Eisner, is visiting Aquarius Information Technologies, France next month.

Could you please ..book..[1] her a single room for ....[2] from Tuesday 2nd September.

If possible, she would like a ....[3] not too far from the AIT office.

..........[4] let us know how much the room ....[5] ....[6], including full breakfast.

Could you please make the ....[7] as soon as you can.

..........[8] you for organising this.

All the best,

Robin Stamford
Aquarius Information Technologies Canada

C **Correct the five errors in Lise's reply. The first one has been done for you.**

To: Aquarius.Infotech@skynetcom.ca
From: Lise.Belfort@aquarius.fr
Subject: Travel arrangements

Dear Robin,

e-mail
Thank you for your ~~fax~~.

We are pleased to confirm that we have booked Mr Eisner in at the Hotel Adagio, which is very near our office.

As you requested, we have booked a double room for two nights from Thursday 2nd September.

The cost is 140 euros, breakfast not included.

With best wishes,

Lise Belfort
Aquarius Information Technologies, France

Food and entertaining

VOCABULARY **A** Choose the best word (a, b or c) to complete the text.

Successful Business Entertaining

Today, you don't .do.¹ business only in your office. All over the world, people understand that it is important to ....² business partners, customers and suppliers. When you plan to go for a ....³ with your visitors, there are a few rules to remember. First, don't take them to a restaurant that nobody knows!

You want a place with a pleasant atmosphere, ...⁴ food and efficient ....⁵. So if you do not know where to go, ask your friends and colleagues to ....⁶ a restaurant.

Secondly, choose a restaurant with a varied ....⁷ so everybody can find a ....⁸ they like or want to try. Remember

too that some of your guests may be ....⁹.

Finally, relax and be open to cultural differences. Some people like a quick lunch or dinner and are very happy with just a main ....¹⁰, but some like to spend more time socialising and also expect an aperitif, starter, main course, dessert, coffee and of course good conversation!

1	**a)** work	**b)** do	**c)** make
2	**a)** entertain	**b)** party	**c)** fun
3	**a)** dish	**b)** menu	**c)** meal
4	**a)** taste	**b)** delicious	**c)** right
5	**a)** chef	**b)** waiter	**c)** service
6	**a)** recommend	**b)** inform	**c)** advise
7	**a)** menu	**b)** card	**c)** bill
8	**a)** food	**b)** dish	**c)** cook
9	**a)** diet	**b)** receipts	**c)** vegetarians
10	**a)** course	**b)** food	**c)** pie

(1 b) do is circled)

B Use the clues to complete the crossword puzzle.

Across

1 'You should try the ..roast.. duck, it's delicious.' (5)
4 Sweet-and-.................... chicken is a Chinese dish. (4)
6 Vegetarians do not eat it. (4)
8 'I'll have the chicken .... as a starter.' (4)
9 A sea fish (4)

Down

2 A world-famous Italian dessert. (8)
3 A very popular type of Italian fast-food. (5)
4 A river and sea fish. (6)
5 Things like apples and bananas. (5)
7 Shall we leave the waiter a ....? (3)

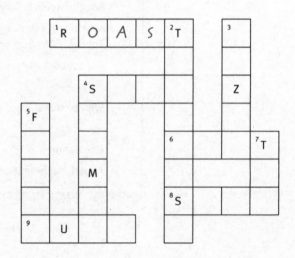

VOCABULARY +

C Match the food words (1–6) to their definitions (a–f). Use a good dictionary to help you.

1 barbecue
2 buffet
3 couscous
4 kebab
5 mousse
6 risotto

a) a dessert made from cream and eggs and often flavoured with chocolate
b) a dish of small pieces of meat and vegetables cooked on a metal stick
c) a meal in which people serve themselves from a table and often eat standing up
d) a typical dish from North Africa made from semolina and often served with meat and a lot of vegetables
e) an Italian dish of rice cooked with vegetables, meat or fish
f) an outdoor meal where food is cooked over an open fire

D Cross out the word that does not normally go with the word in the bubble.

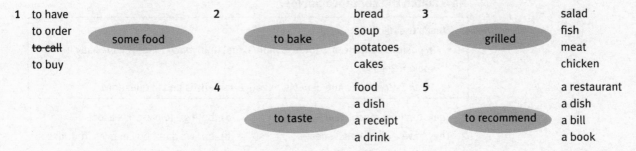

1 to have
   to order
   ~~to call~~
   to buy
   some food

2 **to bake**
   bread
   soup
   potatoes
   cakes

3 **grilled**
   salad
   fish
   meat
   chicken

4 **to taste**
   food
   a dish
   a receipt
   a drink

5 **to recommend**
   a restaurant
   a dish
   a bill
   a book

LANGUAGE REVIEW

Countable and uncountable nouns

A Write the words from the box in the correct column.

~~beef~~ credit card fish hamburger money restaurant soup waiter

Countable		Uncountable	
1	3	5 ...*beef*...	7 ....
2	4	6	8 ....

B Write the sentences (1–9) in the correct place in the table.

	singular countable noun	plural countable noun	uncountable noun
+	1 I'd like a dessert.		
–			
?			

1 ~~I'd like a dessert.~~
2 Are there **any** green apples?
3 I don't want **a** large glass.
4 I'd like **some** chips.
5 I'd like **some** soup.
6 Is there **a** Chinese restaurant in town?
7 Is there **any** meat in it?
8 There are**n't any** tables free.
9 We do**n't** have **any** milk.

LANGUAGE WORK

C **Complete the sentences with *much* or *many*.**

1 How ..*much*.. food do we need for the buffet lunch?

2 There aren't .... rice dishes on the menu.

3 How .... tables do we need to reserve?

4 That's not a very exciting menu. There isn't .... choice, is there?

5 Their food is always excellent, but they don't have .... desserts.

6 Let's go to another restaurant. There are too .... people here.

7 There's too .... salt in this soup. I can't eat it.

8 There isn't .... to do for the staff party. Khalil organises everything.

D **Study these sentences.**

*I drink **a lot of** water.*   *I don't drink **much** milk.*

*We need **a lot of** vegetables.*   *Do we need **many** potatoes?*

Now match the sentence halves.

> **What's the rule?**
> - In positive sentences, *a lot of* is more usual than *much / many*, especially in spoken English.
> - *Much / Many* are more usual in negative sentences and in questions.

1 They don't eat much meat,   a) but I go to pizzerias a lot.

2 They have a lot of fish dishes,   b) but we don't buy many soft drinks.

3 We make a lot of fresh fruit juice,   c) but he never invites many people to his parties.

4 I don't go to Indian restaurants much,   d) but they don't have many starters.

5 He has a lot of money,   e) but we sometimes eat a lot of chocolate.

6 I need a lot of eggs,   f) but I don't need much milk.

7 We don't buy many sweet things,   g) but they eat a lot of vegetables.

WRITING

Editing

A **Read the review of the White Lake Restaurant.**
In each line **1–7** there is **one wrong word**. For each line, **underline the wrong word** in the text and **write the correct word** in the space provided.

You can entertain <u>you</u> guests in a beautiful setting at the White
Lake Restaurant. In the heart of Belleville Forest, just ten minute
away from the city centre by public transport or by car, he has
excellent parking facilities. At a White Lake Restaurant, you can enjoy
delicious fish dish from our region, as well as a wide range of
vegetarian and meet dishes. It is a popular place so you need to
booking a table in advance. It is quite expensive, but it is worth a visit.

1 ......*your*.......
2 ....
3 ....
4 ....
5 ....
6 ....
7 ....

Messages **B** Number the sentences of the telephone message in the correct order.

For: The White Lake Restaurant Manager   From: Liz Arana of Crawley Electronics 01865 896 442

Date: 12th November

a) It's for a group of 18, including 14 Chinese visitors. ☐

b) Ms Arana wants to book one of our dining rooms for Friday evening, 22nd November. ☐ 1

c) So can we do a three-course meal with a lot of regional specialities? ☐

d) We also need to quote her a price (drinks included) before 15th November. ☐

e) The others want to try typical dishes from our region. ☐

f) There are three vegetarians in the group. ☐

E-mails **C** Complete the e-mail with words from the box.

vegetarian   yours   confirm   menu   again   ~~pleased~~   book

Dear Ms Arana

Thank you for your enquiry of 12th November.

We are .pleased.¹ to inform you that you can ....² our exclusive Viennese Dining Room for 22nd November from 7 p.m. It can seat up to 25 people and has a beautiful view of the lake.

You can find a sample ....³ on our website. It has a lot of typical dishes, including some regional fish dishes and ....⁴ specialities. Please let us know what you think.

The price for a three-course meal (vegetarian or standard) would be £40 per person, including drinks and 10 per cent service.

For first-time customers like you, there is a special offer: you can choose anything from our desserts menu completely free of charge, as well as tea or coffee.

Could you please ....⁵ your booking by 17th November.

Thank you once ....⁶ for your enquiry.

We look forward to seeing you and your guests on 22nd November.

.....................⁷ sincerely

J Richards

Restaurant Manager

Buying and selling

LANGUAGE WORK

VOCABULARY **A** Choose the best word (a, b or c) to complete the text.

> When buyers *place*.¹ an order with a seller for the first time, they usually have a lot of questions.
>
> First, they want to ....² prices, of course, and they also want to know what kind of ....³ the seller can offer.
>
> Very often, buyers also ask if the seller has the goods in ....⁴ and if he or she can deliver on ....⁵.
>
> Sometimes, buyers will ask if it is possible to pay in ....⁶. If the seller agrees, he or she will often expect buyers to pay a ....⁷.

1 a) put   b) take   c) place *(circled)*
2 a) compare   b) offer   c) say
3 a) commission   b) discount   c) feature
4 a) shop   b) stock   c) delivery
5 a) delay   b) speed   c) time
6 a) instalments b) parts   c) shares
7 a) deposit   b) cheque   c) guarantee

B Use the clues to complete the crossword puzzle.

Across

2 At Dart Car Hire the ...... *buyer* ...... can get some deals for half price. (5)

4 When you bring the car back, we e-mail you a detailed .... (7)

7 It doesn't cost extra for insurance. It's .... (4)

9 As a Dart Car Hire Gold Club member, you get free hire days or airline miles as your .... (6)

10 Club members also enjoy many other exclusive .... (8)

Down

1 Be quick! Our offer is for a limited .... only. (6)

3 At Dart Car Hire you don't queue when you .... the car – we e-mail you all the information. (6)

5 As a Dart Car Hire Gold Club member, you can .... free hire days or airline miles. (6)

6 You can pay over a 12-month period. We offer interest-free .... (6)

8 If you hire a Mini or a Smart car, you can .... up to 50 per cent. (4)

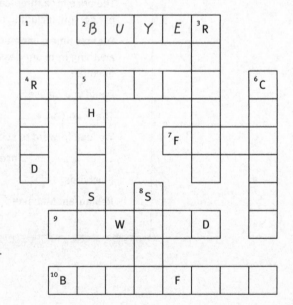

VOCABULARY +
Collocations

C Cross out the word that does not normally go with the word in the bubble.

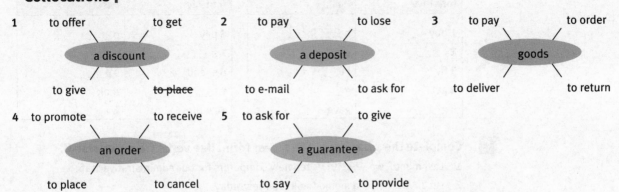

1   to offer   to get
        a discount
    to give   ~~to place~~

2   to pay   to lose
        a deposit
    to e-mail   to ask for

3   to pay   to order
        goods
    to deliver   to return

4   to promote   to receive
        an order
    to place   to cancel

5   to ask for   to give
        a guarantee
    to say   to provide

D Match the words and phrases (1–6) to their definitions (a–f).

1   after-sales service   a) a company or a person that provides a particular type of product
2   guarantee period   b) help, advice or free repairs that you get after you buy a product
3   retail   c) a person who tries to be more successful than you
4   wholesale   d) the selling of goods to businesses, usually in large quantities
5   supplier   e) time when the seller repairs or replaces a product free of charge
6   competitor   f) the selling of goods to the public, usually through shops

E Complete each sentence with a word or phrase from exercise D.

1   Lantex never delivers on time. We have to look for another .supplier.

2   Our products are available in department stores and other .... outlets.

3   Sales are very good, but our main ....'s sales are also going up
    very quickly.

4   Ten per cent discount and a two-year ....! That's a very good offer.

5   We are in the .... trade and sell our clothes to retailers and
    fashion houses.

6   If you have a problem with the machine, just contact our .... department.

LANGUAGE REVIEW
Past simple

A Complete the sentences with *was* or *were*.

1   Sandra .was. at the meeting.

2   Jeff and Liz .... at Head Office yesterday.

3   There .... a lot of sales representatives at the meeting.

4   It .... difficult to get a discount.

5   The people .... nice, but their questions .... very difficult. Or
    maybe I .... just a bit tired.

6   The product presentation .... last Tuesday. My boss and I ....
    there to talk about our new brand of soft drinks.

7   Their products .... always the best on the market.

8   Two or three of our customers from Korea .... there.

LANGUAGE WORK

B Write the missing letters to complete the verb forms.

Infinitive	Past
1 buy	b o u g h t
2 c _ _ _	cost
3 fly	f l _ _
4 get	g _ _
5 g _ _ _	gave

Infinitive	Past
6 pay	p _ _ _
7 s _ _ _	sold
8 spend	s p _ _ _
9 t _ _ _	took
10 write	w r _ _ _

C Complete the sentences with a past form. Use verbs from exercise B.

1 Last month, we .bought. ten new computers for our administrative staff.

2 I..................... a memo to all reps yesterday.

3 He..................... up at 9 o'clock so of course he was late for the meeting.

4 Our company..................... a lot on promotion last year.

5 They..................... for everything in cash.

6 We..................... back to Zurich with Lufthansa.

D Complete the information about the sales figures with the past form of the verbs given.

Last year's overall sales figures .were.[1] excellent for Nielsen Electronics. In January, they ....[2] the RU20 CD player and sales ....[3] up from 2,000 to 2,500 the next month. In March, sales ....[4] 3,500.	be introduce go reach
Sales then ....[5] at the same level through the next quarter, but they ....[6] to go up in July and August, when they ....[7] to 4,000.	stay continue increase
Nielsen ....[8] to launch their digital camcorder, the DCC-N300, in September, but production problems ....[9] the introduction of this new model.	want delay
So Nielsen ....[10] it at the end of October. Overall sales ....[11] down after August and at the end of October they were at 3,500.	launch go
However, the DCC-N300 ....[12] very popular and the overall volume of sales ....[13] until the end of the year, when it ....[14] 4,500.	be grow reach

E Use the information in exercise D to draw the approximate pattern of overall sales.

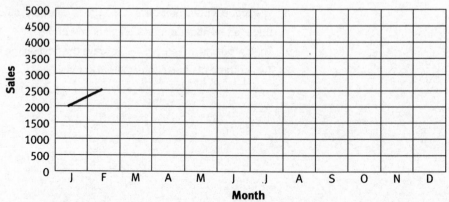

WRITING

Editing

A **Rewrite the sentences with the words from the box in the correct places.**

| a   address   ask   ~~be~~   deposit   for |

1 Salespeople have to clear what their objectives are.
   Salespeople have to be clear what their objectives are.

2 Before they place an order, a lot of people like to questions.
   ....

3 Please quote us price for the goods listed below.
   ....

4 This special promotion is only a short time.
   ....

5 Unfortunately, we wrote the wrong delivery on the package.
   ....

6 We paid a €200 and the rest in 12 monthly instalments.
   ....

B **Read the job advertisement.**

In each line **1–6** there is **one wrong word**.

For each line, **underline the wrong word** in the text and **write the correct word** in the space provided.

We are a medium-sized cosmetics an toiletries company based in Victoria.	1	......*and*......
Last year we increased our sales by 20 per cent and launch several new products.	2	....
At present we are expanding our sale force, creating opportunities throughout	3	....
the country for experience sales representatives. Our sales representatives	4	....
manage their own areas and help customers to promote our brands. They showing	5	....
customers how to increase sales. The advise customers on equipment,	6	....
advertising and special promotions.		

People

VOCABULARY

A Complete the sentences with adjectives about people.

1 Luigi is a very q u i e t person. He never says anything in meetings.

2 I am _ _ _ _ t _ _ _ _ and I would really like to become head of my department one day.

3 Leila is very _ _ _ d-w _ _ _ _ _ _ . She works longer hours than everyone else.

4 Our new manager has lots of new ideas and she always finds good solutions to problems. She's very _ _ _ a t _ _ _ .

5 Heinrich likes going to parties and meeting new people. He's extremely _ _ _ i a _ _ _ .

6 You're late again. Could you try to be a bit more _ _ _ c t _ _ _ ?

B Complete the sentences with words from the box. Write Ø if no word is missing.

| at   for (x2)   on   to   with (x2) |

1 A motivating manager encourages ..Ø.. employees to work well.

2 A sales rep should never be rude .... customers.

3 Yasin is very helpful. He likes to do things .... other people.

4 Sandra always meets .... deadlines.

5 Claudia is very practical. She is really good .... making things work.

6 Sakiko is never late .... meetings.

7 Yeliz likes working in a team and she gets on well .... others.

8 A good employee always arrives .... time.

9 He was nice, but he was not very popular .... his colleagues.

10 Their new manager really knows how to motivate .... staff.

C Match the sentence halves to make definitions for other adjectives about people.

1 A successful person

2 A confident person

3 A knowledgeable person

4 A patient person

5 A polite person

6 A reliable person

7 A smart person

8 An efficient person

a) does not let you down.

b) stays calm when they have to wait for a long time.

c) can do tasks well without wasting time.

d) is dressed in a neat and attractive way.

e) knows a lot about a particular subject.

f) is sure that they can do something well.

g) speaks or behaves in a way that is not rude to other people.

h) can always do what they try to do.

LANGUAGE REVIEW

Past simple: negatives and questions

A **Write the missing letters to complete the verb forms.**

Infinitive	Past		Infinitive	Past
1 begin	b e g a n		6 find	f _ _ _ _
2 b r _ _ _	brought		7 go	w _ _ _
3 catch	c a _ _ _ _		8 know	_ _ _ w
4 come	c _ _ _		9 l _ _ _ _	left
5 _ _ _ _ _	drove		10 send	s _ _ _

B **Complete the sentences with the correct form of verbs from exercise A.**

1 I didn't .know. that you .went. on a training course last month.
2 I didn't .... to work because of the snow. I .... a bus instead.
3 Why did Emma .... the company?
4 Did he .... the report by post or did he .... it here himself?
5 When did the training course ....?
6 Our first manager really .... how to motivate us, didn't he?
7 I didn't .... to the staff meeting. I was feeling very ill.
8 This is very useful information. Where did you .... it?
9 Did you .... the early morning train?
10 Why didn't Peter .... into partnership with Koreka Media?

C **Now match the responses (a–j) to the sentences in exercise B.**

a) He certainly did. We all wanted to work hard for the company. | 6 |
b) He delivered it by hand yesterday afternoon.
c) Well, he heard that they were in financial difficulty.
d) It was all in last year's annual report.
e) No, I didn't. I came by car.
f) On 26th February.
g) Really? I thought everyone in the office knew!
h) Well, I think she didn't get on with the new manager.
i) Were you? Did you see a doctor?
j) Yeah. I left my car at home, too.

Question forms

D **Write the words in the correct order to make questions.**

1 they / punctual / Were / ?
Were they punctual?
2 a / Did / he / in / like / team / to / work / ?
....
3 they / Were / hard-working / ?
....
4 colleagues / her / popular / Mrs Whitehead / Was / with / ?
....
5 motivate / know / Did / how / people / she / to / ?
....
6 happy / Sandra / to / Were / with / work / you / ?
....

E **Match the short answers (a–f) to the questions in exercise D.**

a) Yes, they were. `1`

b) No, she wasn't. ☐

c) Yes, she did. ☐

d) No, he didn't. ☐

e) Yes, I was. ☐

f) No, they weren't. ☐

F **Complete the short answers to the questions.**

1 Was Philip on time? No, *he wasn't*.

2 Did you and Barbara go to the staff party? No, ...

3 Did the sales reps get all the information they need? .... did.

4 Were Sue and Tom in the same team? .... weren't.

5 Does Sue work in the research team? No, ...

6 Was the training course useful? Yes, ...

7 Were the participants satisfied? Yes, ...

8 Can you meet this deadline? Yes, ...

G **Read the text. Then make questions for the answers below.**

Birgitte Nielsen was born in Aarhus, but her parents moved to Copenhagen when she was only three years old.

She was a very successful student. Her favourite subjects were Physics and Maths. In fact, she was always very good with numbers, maybe because her father worked in a bank and her mother was a computer programmer.

At the age of 18, Birgitte wrote a book called FORTRAN for Beginners. The students liked it a lot and said it was better than the course book!

After secondary school, she went to Dublin for a few years, where she did an MBA. Her two passions, computer programming and business, led her to found her own company at the age of 25. Today, Nielsen Electronics is a very successful business, with branches in five different European countries.

1 In Aarhus. *Where was Birgitte born?*

2 To Copenhagen. ....

3 Yes, she was. ....

4 Physics and Maths. ....

5 In a bank. ....

6 Yes, they liked it a lot. ....

7 In Dublin. ....

8 She founded Nielsen Electronics. ....

9 Yes, it is. ....

10 Five. ....

WRITING

Linkers:
because/
but/so

A **Complete the sentences with linkers from the box.**

because (x4)   but (x2)   so (x2)

1 Management is very worried *because* sales are falling.

2 After graduating, Miguel wanted to help his parents .... he worked for a year in the sales department of their company.

3 Leila studied law at university, ... her dream was to find a job in marketing.

4   Our sales went up quickly .... our new products were very successful.

5   Piers was voted salesperson of the year .... he helped increase sales by
    15 per cent.

6   Tamara wanted to improve her English .... she decided to study for a
    diploma in business in Dublin.

7   Vladimir had a permanent position, ... he changed his job after a year
    .... he did not get on with his boss.

Editing   **B**   **Read the first part of a letter of reference.**

In most of the lines **1–8** there is **one extra word** which does not fit. Some lines, however,
are correct.

If a line is **correct**, put a tick (✓) in the space provided.

If there is an **extra word** in the line, write that word in the space provided.

Dear Ms Eastwood

Thank you for your letter of the 2nd February about Marcel Lacour's	1 ....✓........
an application for the job of Deputy Director.	2 ....*an*........
Marcel is worked with us for three years as Office Manager. Then he	3 ....
worked for two years in the same position in the our Paris subsidiary.	4 ....
He has a degree in Accountancy and Management and he is currently	5 ....
doing a part-time MBA. His knowledge of languages includes any	6 ....
French, English, Greek and Polish. This makes him a very suitable	7 ....
for work in a European of organisation.	8 ....

C   **Now match the sentence halves to make the second part of the letter
of reference.**

1   He is an excellent manager,
    very dedicated to the staff

2   He is hard-working and gets

3   He motivates the staff and

4   He is good at dealing with problems
    and is very good at

5   Marcel is completely reliable and always

6   He has a very positive attitude to

7   I highly recommend him

a) is a good team leader.

b) for this post.

c) his work and is a creative and flexible person.

d) negotiating solutions.

e) meets his deadlines.

f) and to the quality of his work.

g) very good results.

Yours sincerely

Julian Ash
Director

Advertising

VOCABULARY **A** **Use the clues to complete the crossword puzzle.**

Across

1 Volkswagen asked Deutsch, L.A. to create a TV commercial to ......*launch*...... its latest car. (6)
4 An .... market is outside the producer's country. (6)
7 Your target market are the people you want to .... at. (3)
8 A .... is a small piece of paper advertising something. (5)
10 .... market products sell to large numbers of people. (4)
12 A .... market is a small, but often profitable market. (5)
13 An American advertising .... created a TV commercial for the 2012 Beetle. (6)
14 The most common .... in advertisements is 'you'. (4)
15 A .... is a short song used in advertising. (6)

Down

1 Ferrari sports cars are a ....-market product. (6)
2 'The world's local bank' and 'I'm lovin' it' are two famous advertising .... (7)
3 'Billboard' is the American English word for '......................'. (8)
5 Advertising on prime .... TV is very expensive. (4)
6 A .... market is in the producer's country. (4)
9 A .... is a special design that a company uses on its products. (4)
11 A free .... is a small amount of a product that a company gives for people to try. (6)
13 '......................' is short for 'advertisement'. (2)

LANGUAGE REVIEW

Comparatives and superlatives

A **Write the missing letters to make the comparative form of the adjectives.**

1 small _e r_
2 larg _ _
3 eas _ _ _
4 hot _ _ _
5 young _ _
6 new _ _
7 big _ _ _
8 happ _ _ _
9 earl _ _ _
10 quiet _ _
11 thin _ _ _
12 nois _ _ _

B **Complete the sentences with the comparative form of words from the box.**

| bad | big | competitive | early | expensive | good | ~~high~~ | young |

1 We spent a lot on Internet advertising last year, but the amount we spent in 2010 was even ..._higher_...

2 We need to think about cost. We all know it's .... to show a commercial on TV in the evening than in the afternoon.

3 Germany is a .... market for cars than Sweden. You can get some real bargains.

4 Sales aren't very good, but don't worry, things could be ....

5 The logo on the T-shirts is too small. It needs to be ....

6 This is not a very good slogan. I'm sure you can think of a .... one.

7 I don't think it's a good idea to wait another month. We need to launch our winter collection .... than our competitors.

8 Our customers are .... and richer than our competitors' customers.

C **Complete the sentences with words from the box.**

| a | difficult | easier | ~~easiest~~ | less | more | most | than | the | worse |

1 I think the ..._easiest_.. mobile to use is the Pronto-X.

2 Is South Korea a .... competitive market than Japan?

3 It is more .... to break into export markets than into home markets.

4 It's not just another good product – it's .... best product on the market.

5 Pete is one of the .... helpful colleagues I have.

6 Sales this month are a bit better .... they were last month.

7 Sales are not going up. We need to find .... better way of entering that market.

8 The design of this model is not very attractive, but it's .... to use than the RL202.

9 The rate of exchange isn't very good this week, but it was even .... last week.

10 Toptek didn't spend much on outdoor advertising and it spent even .... on radio advertising.

LANGUAGE +

much/a lot,
a little/a bit

D **Study these sentences about large and small differences.**

The Chinese market is	**much** **a lot**	more attractive	than the Ukrainian one.
	a little **a bit**	harder to break into	

> **Note**
> *Much* and *a little* are usually preferred in formal, written English.

Read the information about two smartphones. Then match the sentence halves to describe the differences between them.

	Virga M100	Pronto-X
Price	€299	€149
Weight	120 grams	90 grams
Size	6 x 11 x 3 cm	6 x 10 x 2 cm
Special features	Has 20 ringtones Has built-in digital camera Comes with 3 fun games Get €80 of free calls when you buy one!	Has 5 ringtones Has built-in digital camera Comes with 10 fun games Get €40 of free calls when you buy one!

1 The Virga M100 is much
2 The Pronto-X is a lot
3 You get a lot more free calls
4 The Pronto-X is a bit smaller
5 The Virga M100 has a lot
6 The Virga M100 has a lot fewer
7 The Virga M100 is much

a) cheaper than the Virga M100.
b) than the Virga M100; it is only 6 x 10 x 2 cm.
c) heavier. It weighs 120 grams!
d) fun games than the Pronto-X.
e) more expensive than the Pronto-X.
f) more ringtones than the Pronto-X.
g) when you buy a Virga M100.

E **Read the information about a third phone. Then complete the sentences.**

Star 8	Price	€90
	Weight	85 grams
	Size	6 x 10 x 2 cm
	Special features	2 ringtones + €10 of free calls

1 The Star 8 is *a lot cheaper* than the Pronto-X.
2 The Pronto-X is .... heavier than the Star 8.
3 The Virga M100 is .... than the Star 8. It is 6 x 11 x 3 cm.
4 The Star 8 has .... ringtones than the Virga M100.
5 Both the Virga M100 and the Pronto-X are .... the Star 8, which costs only €90.
6 The Star 8 weighs only 85 grams. It is .... the Virga M100.

WRITING
E-mails

A **Complete the e-mail with phrases from the box.**

> ~~for sending~~   like to know   look forward to   please confirm   interested in

Dear Ms Werner

Thank you *for sending* .¹ us the technical information about your range of air conditioners.

We are particularly ....² your Aeolis and Zephyr portable models and plan to buy five of each.

Could you ....³ that you have those items in stock.

As this is a large order, we would also ....⁴ what sort of discount you offer.

We ....⁵ hearing from you.

With best wishes
João Ramos

B **Read the tip. Then number the sentences of the informal e-mail in the correct order.**

Tip
In many e-mails and letters, information is often presented in the following order:
1 greeting
2 thanks / reference to earlier contact
3 most important point
4 other point(s)
5 reference to future contact
6 closing
7 signature

a) Kind regards, ☐

b) I'm looking forward very much to seeing you next week. ☐

c) I'm glad that we'll all be there to agree on the price of our new energy drink and how to promote it. ☐

d) Thanks for sending the agenda for our marketing meeting next Thursday. ☐

e) However, I'd like to suggest that we once again discuss the name of this new product or am I the only one not to be wildly enthusiastic about 'Gulp'? ☐

f) Hi Vicky, [1]

g) Max ☐

C **Rewrite the e-mail using paragraphs, punctuation and capital letters where necessary.**

To:	Tom
From:	Kim
Subject:	Impex account

hi tom mr stankov from impex contacted me this morning he is very unhappy because he hasnt received the samples of our new products he says he may not order from us again could you please send him another box of samples as soon as possible you know russia is a very important market for us and we dont want to lose this customer many thanks for dealing with this best regards kim

Companies

VOCABULARY

A Complete the text with the correct form of verbs from the box.

~~begin~~ export have launch manufacture provide

Sonara .. *began* ..[1] in 1972 near Turin. Today, it ....[2] mainly aircraft engines, but in the 1970s it also ....[3] the car industry with components. It ....[4] a workforce of 2,000.

Sonara...........................[5] 75 per cent of its engines to other European countries. Last month, it ....[6] a new type of engine which burns 15 per cent less fuel than other models.

B Match the sentence halves.

1 Panetti **employs** over 3,500 people,

2 It **introduced** four new products last year,

3 It **makes** bread and

4 Panetti only **supplies** its own shops;

5 It doesn't **sell** any of its products **abroad**,

a) but it plans to expand into France.

b) including 1,400 in its own retail outlets.

c) including sandwiches and pies.

d) many other bakery products.

e) it does not make products for anyone else.

C Match these words and phrases from exercise A with a word or phrase from exercise B that has a similar meaning.

1 manufactures ......*makes*......

2 provides ....

3 has a workforce of ....

4 export ....

5 launched ....

> **Notes**
> *Make* and *manufacture* do not have exactly the same meaning. To *manufacture* means to 'make large quantities of goods in a factory, using machines'. You *manufacture* (or *make*) cars, drugs, plastic goods, etc., but you usually *make* (not *manufacture*) bread, cheese, etc.

D Match the sentence halves.

1 Juliette is in charge

2 Panetti is going to create

3 Alex is responsible

4 They manufacture plastic furniture

5 Jo and Francis are involved

6 She likes to make presentations

a) about future projects.

b) for quality control.

c) in international construction projects.

d) a new product.

e) of a department of 15 staff.

f) under the brand name Tekko.

LANGUAGE REVIEW

Present continuous

A **Write the -ing form of these verbs.**

1 try ....trying....
2 develop ....
3 increase ....
4 run ....
5 stay ....
6 get ....

7 take ....
8 listen ....
9 refer ....
10 manufacture ....
11 work ....
12 happen ....

B **Write λ to show the place of the missing word in each sentence. Write the word on the line.**

1 I λ translating our company's mission statement into Chinese. ......am......
2 We are sorry to hear the new machines not working very well. ....
3 Many foreign companies investing in Turkey. ....
4 Sonara's sales figures improving? ....
5 We looking for a manager with a lot of experience in finance. ....
6 Wilhelm still checking the company accounts? ....
7 Unfortunately, the south of the country not attracting many investors. ....
8 You planning to break into the Brazilian market, aren't you? ....

C **Complete the sentences with the present continuous form of the verbs in brackets. Use the negative where necessary.**

1 Business is not very good this season so we ..aren't recruiting.. any extra staff. (recruit)
2 How about Fadila? Is she at head office or .... she .... from home? (work)
3 We're glad to report that our shops .... very well. (do)
4 Sales are now much better in the east of the country, but they .... in the west. (increase)
5 Don't worry, Mr Lorenz .... to open a new factory. 'No more expansion!' he said. (plan)
6 Who .... with all the paperwork this week? (deal)

D **Complete the short answers to these questions.**

1 Is the situation getting better? Yes, ..it is...............
2 Are Sonara and Alfitel working together now? Yes, ...
3 Are they improving the quality of their services? No, ...
4 Is Mr Robertson looking for a bigger factory? No, ...
5 Are you and Robert testing our new product? Yes, ...
6 Hi Sam! So you aren't working for RTS Sports anymore? No, ...
7 Is Barbara trying to get money for her new project? Yes, ...
8 Is their new shop attracting a lot of customers? No, ...

LANGUAGE WORK

Present simple and present continuous

E **Complete the sentences with the correct form (present simple or present continuous) of the verbs in brackets.**

1 We ..develop.. three or four new products every year. Currently, we .are. developing. a new type of air conditioner. (develop)

2 I think our sales figures .... this May. This is unexpected – normally they .... in autumn and winter. (improve)

3 It generally only .... one year to develop a new product, but the FX200 .... longer because of technical problems. (take)

4 Mrs Wu .... all our product presentations. This week, she .... our next presentation in Vancouver. (organise)

5 This is where we .... our products. As you can see, Martin .... some cosmetics from our latest range. (test)

6 We .... Sonara's laboratory until our new one is ready. Otherwise, we never .... other people's facilities. (use)

F **Complete the sentences with the correct form (present simple or present continuous) of the verbs from the box. Use each verb twice.**

answer   employ   speak   think   translate

1 Ana .is translating. this year's directors' report into Spanish.

2 We .... all our customers' calls politely and efficiently.

3 They .... of expanding into the new markets of Central Asia.

4 Lucy thinks she can get a good job in China because she .... Mandarin.

5 How many people .... the company .... ?

6 Please check this invoice. I .... the figures are wrong.

7 Can you hold? Mr Souayah .... on the other line.

8 Business is so good that we .... an extra 200 staff.

9 Attila .... the phone this week because our secretary is away.

10 We always .... all our company brochures into five languages.

WRITING
Editing

A **Read this information about Shanghai Tang, the Chinese clothing design company.**

In most of the lines **1–10** there is **one wrong word**. Some lines, however, are correct.

If a line is **correct**, put a tick (✓) in the space provided.

If there is a wrong word in the line, **underline the wrong word** in the text and **write the correct word** in the space provided.

Shanghai Tang manufactures and <u>selling</u> designer clothes and fashion accessories	1 ....sells.......
inspired by traditional Chinese culture. The brand's founder, David Tang, is from	2 ....✓...........
Hong Kong. 'We make traditional Chinese clothes and we modernise them,' he say.	3 ....
The company's designers doing a lot of research when they plan a new collection.	4 ....
The clothes are luxurious and elegant, but they are also clothes that people want to	5 ....
wearing because they make them feel special.	6 ....
Shanghai Tang's parent company is the Richemont Luxury Group, which also owns	7 ....
Cartier, Montblanc, Chloé, Jaeger-LeCoultre and several other global brand.	8 ....
Shanghai Tang has its flagship store in Hong Kong's Central District, and its also	9 ....
has stores in cities like Paris, Tokyo, London, New York, Dubai and Zurich.	10 ....

B **Rewrite the letter using paragraphs, punctuation and capital letters where necessary.**

dear sir or madam we are writing to request further information about your new range of trainers we are a large chain of retailers of sportswear we are looking for a manufacturer of footwear for the french market we operate from over 400 stores and always order in large quantities could you please send us details of special discounts for such orders and your latest catalogue we look forward to hearing from you yours faithfully barbara costa

Dear Sir or Madam,
We are ...

Company literature

C **Complete the text with words or phrases from the box.**

as well as   but also   finally   for example   ~~not only~~
the first one   the second one

WELCOME TO RFC GROUP

RFC Group plc is one of the largest financial services companies in the country. It has branches *not only*[1] in the capital, ...[2] in four other cities. RFC is rapidly expanding overseas.

....................[3], it already has operations in Brazil, Poland and Turkey.

RFC has two main divisions.

....................[4] is its Financial Services Division.

This division provides independent financial advice to start-up companies.

....................[5], the Internet Technology Division, provides secure e-mail services ....[6] access to online databases. ....[7], it also has a unit helping small companies design their own websites.

Communication

VOCABULARY **A** **Use the clues to complete the crossword puzzle.**

Across

1   A .briefing. is a meeting where information or instructions are given. (8)

3   Our employees can .... forums or messages boards to communicate with colleagues around the world. (4)

5   It's easy to keep in touch with friends and colleagues by e- .... (4)

8   Mr Colao uses his smartphone to...................... Facebook. (6)

10 A...................... is a knowledge-sharing site. (4)

11 How often do you .... your work e-mails when you are on holiday? (5)

13 .... is a system that allows you to send or receive written messages by mobile phone. (3)

14 You can .... your ideas and comments on our electronic message board. (4)

Down

1   A .... is a web page in which someone writes about their opinions, activities, etc. (4)

2   Conference .... can be very useful for keeping up to date on projects. (5)

4   A .... is a piece of writing that you put on a wall or on a special board to give information to people. (6)

6   When you communicate, do you prefer to meet people ....-to-face or to speak on the phone? (4)

7   Mr Colao often .... ideas and exchanges information with colleagues on his BlackBerry. (5)

9   Facebook, Twitter, LinkedIn and MySpace are popular .... networking sites. (6)

12 .... rooms are great. You can exchange ideas with people around the world. (4)

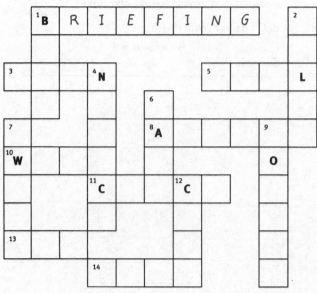

Prepositions **B** **Complete the e-mail with suitable prepositions.**

To:	Alex
From:	Tim
Subject:	Brussels trip

Alex,

Here is your draft programme.

You are leaving ..on..[1] Saturday, 9th June ....[2] 12.40 from Manchester Airport, arriving at Brussels S. Charleroi at 15.05. That's local time so don't worry! You're flying Ryanair, flight number FR3222.

The company driver will meet you ....[3] the airport and take you ....[4] the Métropole Hotel ....[5] the centre of Brussels. ....[6] the hotel it is just a three-minute walk ....[7] the Chamber of Commerce.

Sunday is free, but Mr Vermeulen will certainly invite you out ....[8] dinner. He too likes to be well-prepared ....[9] meetings!

The meetings ....[10] Monday start at 8.30 and will probably go on ....[11] lunchtime, which is 12.15. Lunch is at the Métropole.

At 13.30, Mr Vermeulen is taking you to the 'Communication Technology at Work' event. It will be a great opportunity for networking.

You will have some more free time ....[12] the evening as your return flight leaves at 22.25 (arriving in Dublin at 22.50). Make sure you let the driver know what time you want him to pick you up.

Please confirm ....[13] the end ....[14] the week that these arrangements are OK.

Tim

LANGUAGE REVIEW

Future forms

A **Complete the sentences with the correct form of *be going to* and a verb from the box.**

call complain expand meet put ~~study~~ talk

1 Mark doesn't want to go on the computer skills course now. He *'s going to study* accountancy instead.

2 I don't want to send the contract as an e-mail attachment. I .... it in the post.

3 Business is good. We .... into Central Asia.

4 A: The title of Nikola's presentation is Get Online!
   B: Oh no! .... he .... about communication technology again?

5 The sales figures are bad and I can see that the department .... its target this month.

6 Sandra has the phone numbers of over 100 customers. She .... them one by one for the marketing survey.

7 We're very unhappy about our website and we .... to the guys who designed it.

B **Match the sentence halves to make predictions.**

1 I'm sure the way companies communicate with employees will
2 Call her at 3.30 –
3 We won't have enough money to
4 I think there will be
5 The figures so far aren't very good, so we won't
6 The system has to be more secure,

a) more control over the Internet.
b) or people won't shop online.
c) change a lot in the next five years.
d) meet our target.
e) she'll be in her office then.
f) change all our computers.

C **Complete the sentences with 'll, will or won't.**

1 Anna doesn't like her new boss. She thinks she ..'ll.. change her job soon.
2 I .... have time to go to the trade fair, I'm afraid. There's far too much work at the office!
3 Try to meet your sales target so you .... get a bonus at the end of the year.
4 Next year .... be our 10th anniversary.
5 Liz doesn't have enough information so she .... be able to finish her report on time.
6 Many people .... shop online because they're worried about security.
7 We checked everything carefully. There .... be any problems this time.
8 Think about how customers .... use your website.
9 I can see you're very busy. Don't worry, I .... do it for you.
10 In a few years' time, everyone .... have broadband Internet access.

D **Write ʌ to show the place of the missing word in each item. Write the word on the line.**

1 They ʌ going to redesign their website. .....'re.....
2 'My computer's not working properly.' 'Don't worry. I call our IT specialist.' ....
3 Our visitors from Korea arriving next Thursday at 11.30. ....
4 We can't be sure that people have more free time in 20 years' time. ....
5 Are you going apply for the post of Systems Analyst with GBS Electronics? ....
6 Do you think you be able to come to the conference? ....
7 I can't make it tomorrow morning, I'm afraid. I giving a talk at the trade fair. ....
8 It cost too much to employ an extra IT assistant. ....
9 We are certain Internet security going to get better. ....
10 I have the report on your desk before Friday, I promise. ....

WRITING

Word order

A **Put the words in the correct order to make sentences.**

1 Dave / I think / take / the 9.45 plane / to Glasgow. / will
   I think Dave will take the 9.45 plane to Glasgow.
2 catch / earlier / flight. / He / the / won't
3 8.45. / check / won't / He / in / until
4 He / a / be / hopes / there / won't / delay.
5 Judith / a / book / him / on / will / later flight.
6 She / book / him / early morning / on / the / won't / flight.
7 arrives / at 10.50, / Dave / for the meeting. / he / so / late / won't be

B **Match the sentence halves to make predictions about the future.**

1 Most people will
2 Businesses won't be
3 More and more people will
4 Internet security won't
5 High street banks won't
6 All companies will

a) have a website for their customers and their staff.
b) do their shopping online.
c) disappear, but many people will prefer online banking.
d) able to compete without an online operation.
e) be able to access the Internet from their mobile phones.
f) be a problem anymore.

E-mails

C **Complete the informal e-mails with words and phrases from the box.**

| arriving | delay | early | I should | later |
| leaving | Please | Sorry | ~~Thanks~~ | you'll |

To: travelsection@jeffreys.co.uk
From: Dave.Walton@jeffreys.be
Subject: Travel arrangements

Hi Judith

..Thanks..¹ for making my travel arrangements.

Everything is fine, but you booked me on flight BA 167, ...²
at 8.30. That means ....³ check in at 7.30. ....⁴
find another flight slightly ....⁵. As you know, the meeting
doesn't start until 11.30.

TTYL*

Dave

---

* Text abbreviation for 'talk to you later'.

To: Dave.Walton@jeffreys.be
From: travelsection@jeffreys.co.uk
Subject: Your travel arrangements

Dear Dave

.....................⁶, I forgot you don't like ....⁷ starts very
much! There is, in fact, another flight at 9.45, ...⁸ in Glasgow
at 10.50. I've just checked and I can still book you on it.

The problem is, if there's a ....⁹, ...¹⁰ be late for
the meeting.

What do you think?

Regards

Judith

D **Write Dave's reply to Judith.**
- · Say which flight you want.
- Say <u>why</u> you want either the 8.30 or the 9.45 flight.

Cultures

VOCABULARY

A Choose the best word (a, b or c) to complete the text.

When people hear the word *culture*, they often think about the cultural life, the history or the .customs.[1] of a country. But when you are in business, you also need to think about *company cultures*.

Companies have different *cultures*: they believe in different things, and they have different ways of working. For example, some companies are formal so staff use ....[2] when they speak to each other and they have to wear business ....[3]. Other companies have a system of ....[4] Fridays, when staff can ....[5] anything they like at the end of the week.

Sometimes, there are also big differences in the amount of time ....[6] that staff can get. In some companies, staff get more paid annual ....[7] than in others, for example. Or staff can choose when they start and finish work – a system called '................'[8]. People can start work at 8, 9 or 10 a.m. and finish at 4, 5 or 6 p.m.

Finally, bosses and employees can communicate in many different ways. Some line managers like to get regular written reports, but others prefer ....[9] communication.

1	a) (customs)	b) uses	c) habits
2	a) family names	b) positions	c) business cards
3	a) dressing	b) fashion	c) suits
4	a) formal	b) casual	c) normal
5	a) wear	b) suit	c) dress
6	a) out	b) off	c) away
7	a) weekends	b) benefit	c) leave
8	a) shift work	b) part time	c) flexitime
9	a) back-to-front	b) face-to-face	c) back-to-back

B Complete the sentences.

1 We can't wear what we like at work. We are all in u n i f o r m.
2 Jane is a nurse at the local health centre. This week, she is on the night _ _ _f_ .
3 Is Ricardo looking for a _ _ _ _ -time job or a full-time one?
4 Is 1st January a p _ _ _ _ _ h _ l _ d _ _ in your country?
5 My son is not of school age yet so I'd like to know if the company has any c h _ _ _ c _ _ _ facilities.
6 Sergei is going to take t _ _ _ _ _f for health reasons.
7 What's his job t _ _ _ _ now? Is he 'General Director'?
8 You should learn to speak a little of the local _ _ _ g _ _ g _ before you go.

C Complete the sentences with words from the box.

control	customer	~~innovation~~	performance	trust

1 Shuru Electronics strongly support ..innovation... They always welcome new ideas and are open to change.

2 They want to introduce an incentive scheme for efficient employees to reward good ....

3 We are essentially a ....-focused business, but of course we also pay attention to sales and profit.

4 At Floryval, we empower employees. We really give them a lot of .... over their work.

5 We want relationships between workers and managers to be open and honest. That's why we encourage .... at all levels of our company.

LANGUAGE REVIEW

should/ shouldn't

A Match the sentences (1–8) with the sentences (a–h).

1 I think someone should talk to the boss.

2 He should try to be a bit more punctual.

3 I don't think you should wear formal clothes to the party.

4 Do you think I should buy my hosts a present?

5 She should go on the training course, too.

6 You shouldn't miss any of the meetings.

7 We should develop a better website as soon as possible.

8 You shouldn't ignore customer complaints.

a) I think all our staff need to develop their computer skills.

b) Our online business is really bad.

c) People in this country think it's rude to be late.

d) They're always very kind to me.

e) They're always very useful.

f) We can't work extra hours on Saturday.

g) Take them seriously and deal with them immediately.

h) Most of the guests will be in jeans.

B Complete the sentences with *should* or *shouldn't*.

1 We ..should.. order online. It's faster.

2 We .... be late for meetings. It's rude.

3 You .... say anything about the food.

4 I don't think you .... interrupt the presenter. She'll take questions at the end.

5 I think Sandra .... move to another department. She's not happy in Sales.

6 They .... use children in advertisements. I find it shocking.

7 Do you think I .... apologise for this short delay?

8 I don't think you .... use first names. They have a rather formal company culture.

LANGUAGE WORK

C Complete the text with *should* or *shouldn't*.

Doing business in Japan

People planning to do business in Japan ..*should*..[1] know a few things about the country, its history and its people.

First of all, you ....[2] hire a good interpreter – someone who speaks the language and who knows the customs and traditions.

Many people in Japan shake hands when they meet, but you ....[3] be too fast. You ....[4] wait and see if they offer their hand first.

When somebody gives you their business card, you ....[5] look at it and read it carefully. You ....[6] write on it, because Japanese people think this is very impolite.

Some advice about meetings – you ....[7] worry about silences during a meeting. You ....[8] respect those silences. And finally, remember that you ....[9] make too much eye contact.

could/would

D A business person is entertaining a colleague at home. Complete these conversation extracts with *Could I, Could you* or *Would you*.

1 A: This chocolate mousse is delicious. ..*Could I*.. have some more?

   B: Of course! We made it especially for you.

2 B: .... like a cigarette?

   A: No, thanks. I don't smoke any longer.

3 A: That was a lovely meal. Thank you very much.

   B: .... like tea or coffee?

4 A: .... make a quick phone call, please? My mobile is at home.

   B: Sure! Use the phone in the study. It's quieter in there.

5 A: Now then, about that meeting I missed this morning. .... tell me what it was about?

   B: Well, we just discussed the details of the product launch.

6 A: .... order me a taxi, please. It's getting late.

   B: .... like a lift to the station?

WRITING

Linkers:
and/because/
but/so

A Complete the sentences with words from the box.

| and (x2)   because (x2)   but (x2)   so (x2) |

1 Before I left for South Korea, I learnt to speak a little of the local language ..*and*.. read about the history of the country.

2 We have a formal company culture, ... we always use first names when we speak to each other.

3 I felt uncomfortable .... there was a long silence during the meal.

4 Their employees aren't happy about the changes .... many of them are leaving.

5 Our new boss is OK, ... we don't like the changes he wants to make.

6 The new manager is having a difficult time .... he doesn't understand local culture.

7 I had a lot of training in cross-cultural relations .... I feel prepared to work abroad.

8 In my last job it was more relaxed. People used first names .... there was no dress code.

B You are an employee in a company where many things are changing. You are not happy about some of the changes. Write an e-mail to the Human Resources Manager. Explain what you are unhappy about and ask for an appointment to see her.

Organise your e-mail like this:

1 Start with 'Dear Ms Roberts'.
2 Say one or two positive things about your job and/or the company.
3 Briefly explain your problems. (Choose two or three points from the list or use your imagination.)
4 Ask when Ms Roberts could see you to talk about this in more detail.
5 Close with a suitable ending.

Problems

- you have to wear a uniform at all times
- not enough face-to-face communication
- too many meetings
- fixed working hours
- a lot of paperwork

Topic sentences

C **Match the sentence halves.**

1 Food is important
2 In my country, most people live
3 Most people have small families –
4 Visitors often say
5 School starts early – 7 o'clock! –

a) and most people start work at that time, too.
b) for both young and old people.
c) in flats, not houses.
d) usually one or two children.
e) that we are hospitable.

Note

The sentences in exercise C are used to begin the five paragraphs in exercise D. They tell us something about the topic of each paragraph. That is why they are sometimes called *topic sentences*.

D **Complete the text with the topic sentences from exercise C.**

Notes

a) ......2...... However, many people have a small house in the country. They like to spend their weekends there.

b) .... Only ten years ago, the average was four children. The situation is different now, partly because both men and women want a career.

c) .... We also finish early, and that is good. School is over at 1.30, and a lot of office workers finish at 2 o'clock.

d) .... Many people are happy with just a snack before school or work, but dinner is a special occasion for everyone, every day. It is usually at about 7 o'clock in the evening. We don't eat fast so dinner sometimes goes on until after eight.

e) .... We like meeting new people. We are a small country so we have to be open to the world. Also, tourism is one of our main industries.

LANGUAGE WORK

VOCABULARY **A** Choose the best word (a, b or c) to complete the job advertisements.

Sales Account Manager

(Post Ref. 144ML)

Salary: £24,000 per year

Edinburgh-based company is seeking a person with sales experience to _increase_ [1] sales worldwide and to ....[2] a large department in the clothing industry.

The person will also need to ....[3] communication between our production, sales and marketing departments.

Background in clothing manufacturing essential.

Please contact: Nadia Hassouni athassouni@btinternet.com or telephone 0131 123 7650.

Telesales Executive (Post Ref. B98ML)

Salary: £20,000 per year

Our Telesales Executive will have the ....[4] to make effective phone calls to marketing contacts and to ....[5] business meetings for our clients.

Needs to be able to ....[6] with stress.

Bebop offers excellent training and promotion ....[7].

Call Glen Williams on 020 4456 1090 or e-mail beboprecruit@easynet.co.uk

---

Sales Manager (Post Ref. 231ML)

Salary: £26,000 per year

Conference and Events Company urgently requires a Sales Manager to ....[8] a team of eight telesales executives.

You will ....[9] the team and ....[10] all sales staff and their problems. In addition, you will ....[11] future marketing campaigns and ....[12] a new marketing strategy.

At least three years' management experience necessary.

Contact: Lidia Shiraz, tel: 01260 271288, e-mail: cec@events.co.uk

---

1 a) increase	b) set up	c) lead
2 a) manage	b) train	c) direct
3 a) create	b) plan	c) improve
4 a) interest	b) ability	c) responsibility
5 a) work	b) organise	c) communicate
6 a) cope	b) succeed	c) motivate
7 a) opportunities	b) facilities	c) qualities
8 a) boss	b) lead	c) drive
9 a) apply	b) practise	c) train
10 a) set up	b) deal with	c) look for
11 a) train	b) control	c) plan
12 a) improve	b) develop	c) increase

Tip
- Use *work for* when you talk about the company or organisation where someone is employed.
- Use *work as* + job.
- Use *work in* + kind of activity.
- Also, use *work in* with words like *bank*, *hotel, hospital* or *factory*.

B **Study the examples and the tip. Then complete the sentences with *for*, *as* or *in*.**

Examples:
*Stephen works **for** an engineering company.*
*Gerhard works **as** a receptionist.*
*Sandra works **in** education.*
*Isabelle works **in** a French restaurant.*

1 He has worked ....*as*... an air traffic controller.
2 Have you ever worked .... the food industry?
3 Would you like to work .... mechanical engineering?
4 Sandra's husband works .... the BBC.
5 Are you going to work .... a clothing company in Edinburgh?
6 Rachel is going to work .... a consultant for a design company.
7 At the moment, he is working .... a travel agency.

LANGUAGE REVIEW

Present perfect

A **Complete the sentences with the present perfect form of the verbs in brackets.**

1 ..*Have*.. you ..*known*.. each other for a long time? (know)
2 .... Khalid and Lucien .... jobs frequently? (change)
3 .... Natalia .... several jobs since leaving university? (have)
4 .... Laura and Stella both .... for the same job? (apply)
5 .... you and Tim ever .... difficulties getting along with Mr Dumas? (have)
6 .... you ever .... in Central Asia? (work)

B **Match the answers (a–f) to the questions (1–6) in exercise A.**

a) Khalid hasn't. But Lucien has had three or four different ones already. ☐ 2
b) No, we haven't. We met at a conference only last week, in fact. ☐
c) Yes, I have. I worked in Kazakhstan from 1998 to 2001. ☐
d) Yes, she has. I don't know how many, though. ☐
e) Yes, they have. That's a coincidence, isn't it? ☐
f) Yes, we have. Especially me. ☐

C **Complete the short answers.**

1 A: Has François ever worked in a bank?
  B: No, *he hasn't*.

2 A: Have all the candidates for interview arrived?
  B: Yes, ...

3 A: So you have worked for Nielsen Electronics, is that right?
  B: Yes, ...

4 A: What about these candidates? Have they ever managed a project?
  B: No, ...

5 A: Have you called a job agency?
  B: No, ...

6 A: Have you and Luis received a reply yet?
  B: Well, Luis ...., but I'm afraid I ....

LANGUAGE WORK

D Which of the time expressions (a–j) can be used to complete the two sentences? There are several possible expressions for each sentence.

1 The last time I saw her was .*three months ago* / ....

2 They haven't been very successful .*this year* / ....

a) three months ago
b) this year
c) for the past ten days
d) last week
e) at 9 o'clock
f) yesterday morning
g) so far
h) over the last five years
i) in 2007
j) five minutes ago

Past simple and present perfect

E Complete the telephone conversation with the correct form (past simple or present perfect) of the verbs in brackets.

Rose: Hi, Michelle. I'm calling about our advert for the post of personal assistant. *Has anybody expressed* (*anybody / express*)[1] any interest yet?

Michelle: Yes, it's all going very well. We .... (*receive*)[2] 31 applications so far and yesterday alone about ten people .... (*phone*)[3] for further details of the job.

Rose: Excellent. So how many applicants .... (*you / select*)[4]?

Michelle: Well, I .... (*start*)[5] working on the selection as soon as I .... (*arrive*)[6] this morning. I'm afraid I .... (*not / finish*)[7] yet, but I .... (*already / select*)[8] eight candidates, all with the right qualifications and experience.

Rose: Very good. .... (*you / invite*)[9] them for interview yet?

Michelle: Well, no. I .... (*think*)[10] you'd like to have a look at all the applications yourself first.

Rose: I won't be back in the office until Friday, I'm afraid, so just go ahead, Michelle. You know I trust you 100 per cent!

Michelle: Thanks. OK then. I'll finish selecting candidates and invite them for interview as soon as I .... (*finish*)[11] the conference programme. I .... (*not / have*)[12] time to deal with it yesterday, with all those phone calls.

WRITING
Word order

A Put the words in the correct order to make interview questions.

1 What / do / skills / have / you / ?
What skills do you have?

2 What / strengths / your / are / ?

3 What / time / do / do / free / in / your / you / ?

4 What / work / people / you / of / with / kind / do / well / ?

5 What / greatest / been / achievement / your / has / ?

6 What / job / like / about / did / last / you / your / ?

7 What / in / do / do / to / future / you / the / want / ?

B Answer the questions in exercise A. Use your imagination if you wish.

Job applications

C When people apply for a job, they usually send a covering letter together with their CV. In this letter, they give further information to explain why they think they are suitable for the job. Nadeem Khan is applying for the post of Sales Manager (see page 48). Complete Nadeem's covering letter (sent as an e-mail) with the phrases (a–g).

a) As you will see from my CV,

b) I am very interested in the post you are offering

c) I look forward to hearing

d) ~~I would like to apply for the position~~

e) In addition,

f) Please let me know

g) When I was with Melrose Computers,

To: cec@events.co.uk
From: khan@durham.co.uk
Subject: Post Ref. 231ML

Dear Ms Shiraz

..d..[1] of Sales Manager advertised in *The Telegraph* on 7th September.

...................[2] I have worked as Assistant Human Resources Manager for four years. I am responsible for training for new staff and also for organising problem-solving courses for senior staff. ....[3] I have managed a number of projects for our overseas subsidiaries. This included a training project for local sales staff in Hong Kong.

...................[4] I also gained a lot of experience in telesales and direct sales. ....[5] because I would like to be involved in both telesales and direct sales. I would also like to use my skills as a trainer in a more challenging environment.

...................[6] if there are any other details you need.

...................[7] from you.

Yours sincerely

Nadeem Khan

Talk business

TALK BUSINESS

INTRODUCTION

The aim of this *Talk business* section is to make you more aware of some of the main features of English pronunciation. This will help you understand spoken English more easily. Hopefully, it will also help you discover areas you may need to work on for your spoken English to sound more natural.

THE SOUNDS OF ENGLISH

◀)) 1 **Look, listen and repeat.**

Vowel sounds		Diphthongs	
/ɪ/	quick fix	/eɪ/	play safe
/iː/	clean sheet	/aɪ/	my price
/e/	sell well	/ɔɪ/	choice oil
/æ/	bad bank	/aʊ/	downtown
/ɑː/	smart card	/əʊ/	go slow
/ɒ/	top job	/ɪə/	near here
/ɔː/	short course	/eə/	fair share
/ʊ/	good books		
/uː/	school rules		
/ʌ/	much luck		
/ɜː/	first term		
/ə/	aˈbout ˈCanada		

Consonant sounds

1 Contrasting voiceless and voiced consonants

Voiceless		Voiced	
/p/	pay	/b/	buy
/f/	file	/v/	value
/t/	tax	/d/	deal
/θ/	think	/ð/	this
/tʃ/	cheap	/dʒ/	job
/s/	sell	/z/	zero
/k/	card	/g/	gain
/ʃ/	option	/ʒ/	decision

2 Other consonant sounds

/m/	mine	/n/	net	/ŋ/	branding	/h/	high
/l/	loss	/r/	rise	/w/	win	/j/	year

Tips
- Identify the sounds that you have difficulty recognising or producing and focus mainly on these.
- Add your own key words in the tables above for the sounds you wish to focus on.
- Using the pause button on your CD player will give you time to speak or write when you do the exercises.

USING A DICTIONARY

Any good dictionary today gives you useful information on the pronunciation of individual words. With the help of the *Longman Business English Dictionary* or the *Longman Wordwise Dictionary*, for example, you will be able to work out the pronunciation of any English word on your own once you are familiar with the phonetic symbols above.

In addition, the dictionary also gives you essential information about *word stress*. When a word has more than one syllable, we always put more stress on one of the syllables, i.e., we speak that syllable more strongly. Look at the dictionary entry for *compete*:

com·pete /kəmˈpiːt/ *v* [I] to try to win something or to be more successful than someone else:

- The ˈ sign shows you that the syllable immediately after it should be stressed: comPETE. You will find various exercises on word stress in Units 1, 5, 6, 8 and 11.

- The : sign shows you that the vowel is long. The contrast between *long* and *short* vowels is very important for mutual understanding. In Unit 5, for example, you will find an exercise on /ɪ/ and /iː/, while Unit 12 has an exercise on /ɒ/ and /ɔː/.

- The · sign is used to separate the syllables in a word.

SOUNDS AND SPELLING

In English,
a) the same sound can be spelt in different ways,
b) the same letters can be pronounced in different ways.

a) Consider for example /əʊ/, the sound of *go slow*. It can be spelt o as in *open*, oa as in *loan*, oe as in *toe*, ough as in *although*, ow as in *know*, or eou as in *Seoul*.

b) Take the letter *u* for instance. It can be pronounced /ʌ/ as in *cut*, /ʊ/ as in *full*, /ɜː/ as in *turn*, /ɔː/ as in *sure*, /juː/ as in *tune*, or /ɪ/ as in *busy*.

Put the following words under the correct sound in the table below (the letters in bold show the sound).

advice	chair	friendship	insurance	million	their
break	conscious	heart	knowledge	said	train
buyer	Europe	height	laugh	scientific	want

Vowels		
/ɒ/	/e/	/ɑː/
1 job	1 sell	1 card
2	2	2 ....
3	3	3 ....

/eɪ/	/eə/	/aɪ/
1 pay	1 share	1 price
2	2	2 ....
3	3	3 ....

Consonants		
/ʃ/	/s/	/j/
1 option	1 sell	1 year
2	2	2 ....
3	3	3 ....

Sound–spelling relationships are explored in Units 1, 2, 3, 4, 5 and 6.

SHADOWING

Shadowing is a very effective way to make the most of the recorded material.
1 Play a short section, i.e. a few words or one line of a dialogue, then pause.
2 Without speaking, repeat internally what you heard.
3 Play the same section again. Pause and speak the words in exactly the same way and at the same speed. Repeat this step until you are completely satisfied with your performance.
4 Play the same section again and speak along with the voice on the recording. This is shadowing.
5 Move on to the next short section of the recording and repeat the same procedure.

Introductions

INDIVIDUAL SOUNDS

A 🔊 2 **Listen to how the letters in bold are pronounced in these words. Do they sound the same (✓) or different (✗)?**

1	**G**erman	**T**urkish	✓	5	**R**ussian	Ku**w**aiti
2	Fran**ce**	**J**apan	✗	6	Engl**a**nd	**I**taly
3	**P**oland	**O**man		7	Brazili**a**n	**A**merican
4	**Sw**edish	**Gr**eek				

🔊 2 **Check your answers. Then listen again and practise saying the words.**

B 🔊 3 **Listen to these words. Notice the sound changes.**

France	French	Denmark	Danish
/ɑː/	/e/	/e/	/eɪ/
Spain	**Spanish**	**Wales**	**Welsh**
/eɪ/	/æ/	/eɪ/	/e/

🔊 3 **Listen again and practise saying the words.**

CONNECTED SPEECH

C 🔊 4 **Listen to the way certain words can be linked.**

an engineer   She's an engineer.

a sales assistant   He's a sales assistant in a supermarket.

What's the rule?

When a word finishes with a **consonant** sound and the word immediately after begins with a **vowel** sound, we usually link those two words.

D **Show where similar links could be made in these sentences.**

1 Azim is an Uzbek airline pilot.   2 Jameel, meet Eric. He's in Accounts.

3 Anita has a lot of interests outside work.   4 This is Olga. She works for us

5 Liz works as a chemist for an Irish company.   in Odessa.

🔊 5 **Listen and check your answers. Then listen again and practise saying the sentences.**

STRESS AND INTONATION

E 🔊 6 **Listen to these words. Notice the stressed syllables.**

Bra·<u>zil</u>   Bra·<u>zil</u>·ian   The stress is on *the same* syllable.

<u>Chi</u>·na   Chi·<u>nese</u>   The stress is on *a different* syllable.

F 🔊 7 **Listen and underline the stressed syllables, as in exercise E.**

1 She's from A·mer·i·ca.   She's A·mer·i·can.

2 He's from It·al·y.   He's I·tal·ian.

3 They're from Brit·ain.   They're Brit·ish.

4 I'm from Ja·pan.   I'm Jap·a·nese.

5 We're from Can·a·da.   We're Ca·na·di·an.

6 It's from Pol·and.   It's Pol·ish.

7 So you're from Hun·ga·ry.   So you're Hun·gar·i·an.

🔊 7 **Check your answers. Then listen again and practise saying the sentences.**

INTRODUCING YOURSELF AND OTHERS

A **Match the sentences (1–10) with the responses (a–j).**

1 Hello.
2 Nice to meet you, Tim.
3 This is Andrea. She's in Marketing.
4 How's business?
5 Are you in Marketing, too?
6 See you later.
7 How about some tea?
8 Business is not very good.
9 Are you from Argentina?
10 Is your company Swiss?

a) Pleased to meet you, Andrea. I'm Liz.
b) No, it isn't. It's French.
c) Hi!
d) Oh, thanks. I'd love some.
e) Yes, I am. I live in Buenos Aires.
f) And you.
g) No, I'm not. I'm in Human Resources.
h) Fine, thanks.
i) Right. Bye now!
j) Oh, I'm sorry to hear that.

B **Complete the conversation with words from the box.**

| are | how's | I'm | manager | meet | ~~name's~~ | pleased | Sales |

A: Hello. My ......*name's*......¹ Francis – Francis Wells. ....² the new accountant.

B: Hi! I'm Tom Murphy. Nice to ....³ you, Francis.

A: ....⁴ to meet you, Tom. ....⁵ you in Accounts, too?

B: No, I'm not. I'm in ....⁶. I'm Assistant Sales ....⁷.

A: Mm, that's interesting. And ....⁸ business?

B: Not too bad.

🔊 **8 Listen and check your answers. Then listen again and practise Speaker B's part.**

LISTENING PRACTICE

C 🔊 **9 Listen and tick the best response, a), b) or c), for each question you hear.**

1 a) Yes, I am.
   b) No, he's Russian.
   c) Yes, he is. ✓

2 a) Yes, I work in Marketing.
   b) Yes, it's in Finland.
   c) This is my mobile phone.

3 a) No, I'm not. I'm a househusband.
   b) Yes. I live and work in Grenoble.
   c) Yes, she is.

4 a) Pleased to meet you, too.
   b) Well, I'm interested in travel.
   c) Yes and I have two children.

5 a) Yes. Her name's Louisa.
   b) No, my brother's an engineer.
   c) Not too bad, thanks.

6 a) No, they're Japanese.
   b) Yes. They're from Osaka, in fact.
   c) They like soccer.

7 a) Yes. We drink a lot of coffee.
   b) Me too.
   c) Thanks very much. I'd love one.

8 a) No, it isn't. It's Swiss, actually.
   b) I'm from Stuttgart. How about you?
   c) No. They're research analysts.

UNIT 2 | Work and leisure

INDIVIDUAL SOUNDS

A ◀)) **10 Listen to the difference between /ɪ/ and /aɪ/.**

/ɪ/	/aɪ/
sit	site
fill	file

B **Put the words from the box into the correct column according to the pronunciation of the letter(s) in bold.**

Swiss   client   cycling   business   design   arrive   office   dinner

/ɪ/ as in quick fix	/aɪ/ as in my price
....	....
....	....
....	....
....	....

◀)) **11 Listen and check your answers. Then listen again and practise saying the words.**

C ◀)) **12 Listen to how the verbs are pronounced.**

one syllable	likes	works
two syllables	o•pens	watch•es
three syllables	tel•e•phones	fin•ish•es

1	travels	..........2..........	5	delivers	....
2	discusses	....	6	visits	....
3	starts	....	7	changes	....
4	closes	....	8	completes	....

D ◀)) **13 Listen to the recording. How many syllables do you hear?**

◀)) **13 Listen again and practise saying the words.**

CONNECTED SPEECH

E ◀)) **14 Listen to the way certain words can be linked.**

a large‿office   in‿a large‿office   He works‿in‿a large‿office.

What's the rule?

When a word finishes with a consonant sound and the word immediately after begins with a vowel sound, we usually link those two words.

F **Show where similar links could be made in these sentences.**

1 He works until eight o'clock.
2 He's interested in advertising.
3 She gets up at six and does exercises.
4 She does a lot of overtime.
5 He has a lot of meetings in the afternoon.

🔊 15 **Listen and check your answers. Then listen again and practise saying the sentences.**

QUESTIONS AND ANSWERS

A **Complete the interview with the questions (a–f).**

a) How often do you have breaks?
b) What hours do you work?
c) ... So, what's your job?
d) When and where do you have lunch?
e) What do you not like about your job?
f) And what exactly do you do?

Interviewer: ....C.......... 1
Ana Ross: I'm Assistant Project Manager.
Interviewer: 2
Ana Ross: I spend a lot of time with our clients. I make a lot of phone calls and I write lots of e-mails.
Interviewer: 3
Ana Ross: Well, it's a nine to five job, but I usually arrive at 8.30 and I often stay until six, sometimes later.
Interviewer: 4
Ana Ross: When I'm not too busy, I sometimes have a short coffee break at 10.30 and at 3.30. And then there's lunch, of course.
Interviewer: 5
Ana Ross: Lunch is at 12.45. I never miss it! Our cafeteria is very good.
Interviewer: 6
Ana Ross: The hours are too long, but it's all right. I love my job and my colleagues are fantastic.

LISTENING PRACTICE

B 🔊 16 **Read the questions (1–10). Then listen and choose the best response, a), b) or c), for each question.**

1 How often do you write reports? `c`
2 Do you travel a lot for work?
3 What time do you usually finish?
4 What do you like best about your job?
5 How's business?
6 Are you from Estonia?
7 What do you do in your free time?
8 How many hours a week do you work?
9 How often do you have meetings?
10 What do you want from work?

SURVIVAL BUSINESS ENGLISH

Problems

INDIVIDUAL SOUNDS

A ◀》 **17 Listen to how the letters in bold are pronounced in these words.**

| late   want   carry   can't |

B ◀》 **18 Listen and complete the words.**

/eɪ/ as in play safe	/ɒ/ as in top job	/æ/ as in bad bank	/ɑː/ as in smart card
1 d a n g e r o u s	4 ___ l i t y	7 _ r _ v e l	10 h _ _ d
2 s _ _ c e	5 w _ _ c h	8 _ _ g	11 _ _ _ t
3 g r _ _ t	6 _ _ f t	9 n _ _ _ o w	12 f _ s _

◀》 **18 Listen again and practise saying the words.**

C ◀》 **19 Listen to these words. Then complete the sentence.**

manager   package   damaged

In these words, the second letter *a* is pronounced / .... / as in .... (See page 52.)

CONNECTED SPEECH

D ◀》 **20 Listen to how *do you* is pronounced in these questions.**

Do you live in a city?   How often do you travel abroad?

Do you go to meetings?   What do you do?

> **Tip**
>
> In informal speech, *do you* (two words) is often pronounced /djə/. That's why it often sounds like one word.

E ◀》 **21 Listen and complete the questions.**

1   Do you .... to work?

2   What time .... you start work?

3   When do .... finish work?

4   Who do you .... to?

5   .... do you do so much overtime?

◀》 **21 Listen again and practise asking the questions.**

STRESS AND INTONATION

F ◀》 **22 Listen to these questions. Notice the stress on the two important words.**

Do you <u>work</u> in an <u>office</u>?

Do you <u>travel</u> a <u>lot</u>?

G **Mark the two main stresses in these questions.**

1   Do you work in August?

2   Do you socialise with colleagues?

3   Do you like your job?

◀))) **23 Listen and check your answers. Then listen again and practise asking the questions.**

WHAT'S THE PROBLEM?

A ◀))) **24 Listen and complete the sentences about problems.**

1 I think there's *something* wrong with their telephone. The line is engaged all the time.

2 The coffee .... is broken. Let's get a new one.

3 We'll have to walk, I'm afraid. The .... is out of order.

4 I can't do the photocopying. There isn't any A4 .... Where can I get some?

5 There's a problem with the invoice. The figures are ....

6 There are no instructions in the package and one piece is ....

B **Number the sentences of the telephone conversation in the correct order.**

a) Goodbye. ☐

b) Good morning. Belco Electronics. How can I help you? ☐ 1

c) It's flat 3, 18 Duke Road. ☐

d) Oh, I'm very sorry to hear that. It's the Max 3000 you bought yesterday, is it? ☐

e) Right. I've got that. I'll put an instruction manual in the post for you straightaway. And once again, sorry about our mistake. ☐

f) Good morning. Steve Jenkins here. Well, it's about the Max 3000 computer software. I'm afraid there are no instructions in the box. ☐

g) Thank you very much. Goodbye. ☐

h) Well, Mr Jenkins, just give me your address and I'll send you the instructions. ☐

i) Yes, that's right. ☐

◀))) **25 Listen and check your answers. Listen again and practise Steve's part.**

LISTENING PRACTICE

C ◀))) **26 Listen and tick the best response, a), b) or c), for each item you hear.**

1 a) Speaking. How can I help you? ✓
  b) No, thanks. Not today.
  c) Yes, of course. What's the model number?

2 a) Well, my air conditioner is out of order, too.
  b) I know. It's a very good machine.
  c) I'm sorry to hear that. What seems to be the problem?

3 a) Is the printer broken?
  b) Could you give us some details, please?
  c) All your invoices are incorrect.

4 a) Yes. I finish work at 6.30.
  b) The instructions are missing and some parts are broken.
  c) I'm sorry. All the trains are delayed. It's terrible!

5 a) Well, I think they're unhappy here. That's the problem.
  b) I don't think there's enough space.
  c) Because they don't go to meetings.

6 a) I'm afraid she's in a meeting just now. Would you like to leave a message?
  b) I'm sorry to hear that.
  c) Hello. Bob Lyons here. I'd like to speak to the manager, please.

SURVIVAL BUSINESS ENGLISH

SOUND WORK

A ◀)) **27 Listen to how the letters in bold are pronounced in these words.**

air**p**ort co**ll**ect h**o**me m**o**ney **o**ffice

B **Put the words in exercise A in the correct column according to the pronunciation of the letters in bold.**

/ə/ as in about Canada	/əʊ/ as in go slow	/ɒ/ as in top job	/ɔː/ as in short course	/ʌ/ as in much luck
....	....	....	....*airport*....	....
....	....	....	....	....

C **Put the words in the box in the correct column in exercise B according to the pronunciation of the letters in bold.**

come **c**onfirm h**o**tel pass**p**ort **sh**op

◀)) **28 Check your answers. Then listen and practise saying the words.**

D ◀)) **29 Listen to the recording. Are the sentences positive (+) or negative (−)?**

1 ....+........	5 ....
2 ....−........	6 ....
3	7 ....
4	8 ....

> **Note**
> You can <u>come</u>.   They <u>can't go</u>.
> The underlined words are stressed.

◀)) **29 Check your answers. Then listen again and practise saying the sentences.**

E ◀)) **30 Listen and complete these polite requests.**

1 Can I ....*use*........ the phone, please?
2 Can I have a ...., please?
3 Can I have the ...., please?
4 Can I have a glass of ...., please?
5 Can I take one of these ...., please?
6 Can I .... an alarm call at 6.15, please?

◀)) **30 Listen again and practise the polite intonation used by the speakers.**

**USING STRESS
TO CORRECT
INFORMATION**

A ◀)) **31 Listen and complete these telephone conversations.**

1 A: So the first name is spelt F-R-A-N-C-I-S.

B: No. It's ....

2 A: And the phone number is 3228 5959.

B: Sorry, no. It's ....

3 A: Ms Salgado's flight number is IP3208.

B: Can you check that again, please? The number I have here is ....

◀)) **31 Listen again and notice how Speaker B uses stress to correct
Speaker A.**

No. It's F-R-A-N-C-E-S.

Sorry, no. It's 3228 5859.

The number I have here is IB3208.

B **Look at the telephone conversations. Underline the part that Speaker B will
stress to correct Speaker A.**

1 A: So you need two single rooms for three nights, from the twenty-third of
   this month?

B: No. We need them from the twenty-first.

2 A: Right. One double room with a shower for two nights.

B: Sorry. I'd like one with a bath, if possible.

3 A: ... and an aisle seat for Ms Sandra Davis. D-A-V-I-S ...

B: Sorry, no. D-A-V-I-E-S.

4 A: The train leaves from platform eighteen, is that right?

B: No sir. You want platform sixteen for Newcastle.

5 A: Is the fitness centre on the ground floor?

B: No, madam. It's on the fourth floor.

6 A: Let me just write this down ... Two hundred and fifty euros and ...

B: Sorry, no. That's two hundred and thirty euros.

◀)) **32 Listen and check your answers. Then listen again and practise
Speaker B's replies.**

**LISTENING
PRACTICE**

C ◀)) **33 Read the questions (1–10). Then listen and choose the best
response, a), b) or c), for each question.**

1 What time does his train arrive?   **b**

2 Is it a room with a good view of the sea?

3 Can I use the phone, please?

4 How far is it from the airport to the hotel?

5 Are there any flights to Vancouver after eight?

6 Do you have any rooms?

7 Can I have a receipt, please?

8 What's the flight number?

9 Can I have an alarm call at 5 a.m., please?

10 Which terminal do Qatar Airways flights leave from?

SURVIVAL BUSINESS ENGLISH

Food and entertaining

SOUND WORK

INDIVIDUAL SOUNDS

A 🔊 **34 Listen to the difference between /ɪ/ and /iː/.**

/ɪ/	/iː/
Tim	team
sit	seat

B **Put the words from the box into the correct column according to the pronunciation of the letter(s) in bold.**

| bill   meal   business   chicken   receipt   Sweden   sweet   manager |

/ɪ/ as in quick fix		/iː/ as in clean sheet	
....	....	....	....
....	....	....	....

🔊 **35 Check your answers. Then listen and practise saying the words.**

CONNECTED SPEECH

C 🔊 **36 Listen and complete the sentences.**

1 It's ....*for*............ you.
2 How about .... dessert?
3 Why don't we invite them .... dinner?
4 Would you like .... more juice?
5 How much time do you have .... lunch?
6 There aren't a lot .... restaurants in this area.
7 What do you recommend .... the main course?
8 They have a lot .... fish dishes on the menu.

Tip

We normally use the weak forms /fə/, /səm/ and /əv/ when *for, some* or *of* are within the sentence.

🔊 **36 Listen again and practise saying the sentences.**

STRESS AND INTONATION

D **Look at the example and explanation. Then underline the word which has a different stress pattern in each line (1–5).**

Example: spaghetti   fajitas   <u>hamburger</u>

Explanation: We say spaGHEtti and faJItas (stress on the second syllable) but
                          HAMburger (stress on the first syllable).

1 service   receipt   menu
2 dessert   salad   starter
3 moussaka   aubergine   tomato
4 popular   average   delicious
5 equipment   quality   customer

🔊 **37 Check your answers. Then listen and practise saying the words.**

EATING OUT **A** **Dieter is taking Bob, a colleague from England, out to dinner in Frankfurt. Complete Dieter's questions with words and phrases from the box.**

Are	~~Do you~~	how about	How's	Shall	Shall we	would you	you like

1 ....*Do you*.... like Italian food?

2 .... I ask for a menu in English?

3 .... you ready to order?

4 What .... like for the main course?

5 .... your food?

6 Now, Bob, ... a dessert?

7 Would .... to have coffee or tea?

8 Right. .... get the bill?

◀)) **38 Listen and check your answers.**

B **Match each of Bob's answers to one of Dieter's questions in exercise A.**

a) I think I need a few more minutes.   3

b) Mm, yeah. I'd love an espresso, actually.   ☐

c) Mm. Some lasagne would be nice.   ☐

d) No, thanks. I don't really like sweet things.   ☐

e) No, that's all right, thanks. I need to practise my German a bit. ☐

f) Oh yes, I love it.   ☐

g) Yes, let's. It's getting late.   ☐

h) Very nice, thank you. We must come here again next time I'm in Frankfurt. ☐

◀)) **39 Listen and check your answers. Then listen again and practise Dieter's part.**

LISTENING PRACTICE **C** ◀)) **40 A businessman is entertaining some colleagues at home. Listen and tick the best response, a), b) or c), for each question you hear.**

1 a) It's delicious.
   b) Yes, thanks, that's fine. ✓
   c) I say enough is enough.

2 a) No. Give me more meat.
   b) Yes, please.
   c) Ice with fish? No, thanks.

3 a) Erm ... Some mineral water would be nice.
   b) No, thanks. I'm fine.
   c) I want some fruit juice.

4 a) I like fish, but I don't like eggs.
   b) Just a little, please. It's delicious.
   c) OK.

5 a) Yes, there's enough for everybody.
   b) No, but we have orange juice.
   c) Yes, of course. Here you are.

6 a) No, thanks. It was lovely, but I'm full.
   b) Yes, of course.
   c) Oh no, please.

Buying and selling

INDIVIDUAL SOUNDS

A **Match the past forms which contain the same sound.**

1	grew	a) cost
2	bought	b) met
3	gave	c) knew
4	got	d) caught
5	said	e) paid
6	sold	f) put
7	took	g) wrote

◀)) 41 **Listen and check your answers. Then listen again and practise saying the words.**

Note
- *are/'re* is often pronounced /ə(r)/.
- *was* is often pronounced /wəz/.
- *were* is often pronounced /wə(r)/.

B ◀)) 42 **Listen and complete the sentences with the form of the verb *to be* that you hear.**

1 Delivery.........'s.........free.
2 There .... no extra cost.
3 How much .... they?
4 It .... a great deal.
5 They .... at the office.
6 We .... away on business.
7 These models .... easy to use.
8 The design .... interesting.
9 We .... looking for experienced sales reps.
10 They .... on time.

STRESS AND INTONATION

C **Put the verbs from the box into the correct column according to their stress pattern.**

advised expanded exported finished improved launched needed
offered promoted received stopped worked

1 O talked	2 O o started	3 o O increased	4 o O o invited
....	....	advised	....
....	....	....	....
....	....	....	....

◀)) 43 **Listen and check your answers. Then listen again and practise saying the words.**

SALES TALK **A** 🔊 **44 Listen to these extracts from product presentations and complete the sentences.**

1 The Tex23 is our most ..*popular*.. laptop computer bag. It's .... for the business traveller and it's available in black or dark brown leather.

2 LockIt is an excellent protection against car crime. It's .... of steel and is very strong.

3 With our new Medico testing kit, busy executives get useful and .... information about their health. It's .... to use because it's fully automatic and it's so small you can carry it in your briefcase.

4 The Dual EM mobile phone is in the low price ...., but it has a lot of special .... For example, you can read and write e-mail messages anywhere in the world.

5 Made for busy office people, the Exex desk chair is .... and very well designed. Exex is the solution to your back problems.

6 With the Storage Wizard you can find any of your CDs or CD-ROMs quickly and easily. It's a very .... storage system that saves a lot of .... and a lot of time.

LISTENING PRACTICE **B** 🔊 **45 A salesperson is answering some customers' questions. Listen and tick the best response, a), b) or c), for each question you hear.**

1 **a)** No, but you can pay a deposit.
   b) Yes. Six per cent on large orders.
   c) Yes. It's one year on all models. ✓

2 **a)** Yes. So we could deliver any time this week.
   b) They are very good indeed – the best on the market.
   c) Well, I'll contact you again tomorrow.

3 **a)** Yes, if you can give us a ten per cent discount.
   b) Yes, of course. But then there's a ten per cent deposit to pay.
   c) I'm afraid those models are no longer in stock.

4 **a)** It's available in small, medium or large.
   b) We can deliver it within three days.
   c) We stock it in white, green and blue.

5 **a)** Yes, they always deliver on time.
   b) Yes. It's waterproof.
   c) €400, delivery included.

6 **a)** Yes, of course.
   b) No, we don't need to compare prices.
   c) Well, they're in the medium price range.

7 **a)** It's for anyone who wants a healthy lifestyle.
   b) Exactly. It's a very competitive market.
   c) It's for a limited period only.

8 **a)** The delivery date was Thursday.
   b) The trade price was €240.
   c) We offer free delivery within ten days.

SURVIVAL BUSINESS ENGLISH

SOUND WORK

GROUPS OF CONSONANTS

A 🔊 46 **Listen and write the missing letters to complete the words.**

1 s 𝒫 end   _ _ _ead   _ _ _ing
2 _ _aff   _ _ _ess   _ _ _ong
3 _ _ill   _ _ _een   _ _i_ _
4 _ _a_ _ical   _ _o_ _em   _ _a_ _ise
5 he_ _ _ul   pu_ _ _ual
6 i_ _ _ease   e_ _a_ _

Tips

Many English words have groups of two or three consonants at the beginning, in the middle or at the end of words. Pronounce those consonants clearly together, without adding any other sound before or between them.

🔊 46 **Check your answers. Then listen again and practise saying the words. Pay attention to the groups of consonants.**

CONNECTED SPEECH

B 🔊 47 **Listen to the way certain words can be linked.**

an‿office   in‿an‿office   He works‿in‿an‿office.

C **Show where similar links could be made in these sentences.**

1 I met Ivan in August.   4 He had a lot of interesting ideas.
2 I didn't send it out on time.   5 Yasmin gets on well with all of us.
3 It wasn't a good idea to sell it.

🔊 48 **Listen and check your answers. Then listen again and practise saying the sentences.**

D 🔊 49 **Listen and complete the short answers.**

1 Yes, he ......*was*...... .   4 No, we ....
2 No, she ......*didn't*...... .   5 No, ...
3 Yes, they ....   6 Yes, ...

🔊 49 **Listen again and practise saying the short answers.**

STRESS AND INTONATION

Tip

In *wh-* questions, the voice often goes down at the end.

E 🔊 50 **Listen to these questions. Notice which words are stressed and also notice how the voice goes down at the end of the question.**

1 How did you get to the office?   4 How old were they?

2 Where did she start her journey?   5 How far was it?

3 When did they found the company?

🔊 50 **Listen again and practise saying the questions.**

MANAGEMENT ISSUES

A **Complete the sentences with words from the box.**

| ~~costs~~ down leave manage suggestion too |

1 I think we should try and keep .... *costs* ...... down.
2 There's .... much work for the staff.
3 Sales are .... again this month, I'm afraid.
4 The problem is, she doesn't know how to .... people.
5 Can I make a ....? I think we should hire some more staff.
6 I think he should .... the company. He's making everyone unhappy.

B **Match the responses (a–f) to the sentences in exercise A.**

a) Everybody says so. And she doesn't support her staff at all. ☐ 4
b) I agree. We are spending far too much. ☐
c) I know they work very hard, but we don't have the money to employ more people, I'm afraid. ☐
d) That's a good idea. Two or three part-time workers would make life easier for us. ☐
e) Yeah. Every day there are complaints about his behaviour. ☐
f) Yes. Business is bad. ☐

LISTENING PRACTICE

C 🔊 51 **Listen to eight extracts from negotiations and decide what each speaker is doing.**
- Write one letter (a–d) next to the number of the speaker.
- Use each letter twice.

Speaker 1: ....
Speaker 2: ....
Speaker 3: ....
Speaker 4: ....
Speaker 5: ....
Speaker 6: ....
Speaker 7: ....
Speaker 8: ....

a) Describing a problem
b) Responding
c) Making a suggestion
d) Explaining the reasons

D 🔊 52 **Read the sentences (1–6). Then listen and choose the best response, a), b) or c), for each sentence.**

1 Why was Daniel so difficult to work with? ☐ a
2 I need support to do my job. ☐
3 Does Peter give his colleagues any problems? ☐
4 Your staff are off sick all the time. What's the problem? ☐
5 There's a lot of work. I really need an assistant. ☐
6 We simply don't have enough staff. ☐

SURVIVAL BUSINESS ENGLISH

UNIT **8** | # Advertising

SOUND WORK

INDIVIDUAL SOUNDS

Tip

Notice that non-stressed syllables often contain the *schwa* sound (/ə/).

A 🔊 53 **Listen to the *schwa* sound (/ə/) in these words (see page 52).**

o O	o O o	O o o
pro•mote /ə/	a•ttract•ive /ə/	qual•it•y /ə/
suc•cess /ə/	con•sum•er /ə/ /ə/	hol•i•day /ə/

🔊 53 **Listen again and practise saying the words.**

CONNECTED SPEECH

Tip

Notice that the ending -er is pronounced /ə/ and *than* is pronounced /ðən/.

B 🔊 54 **Listen to the *schwa* sound in these comparative forms.**

1 better — better than — It's better than last month.
2 cheaper — cheaper than — Life is cheaper here than in Paris.
3 heavier — heavier than — This model is heavier than the RT100.

🔊 54 **Listen to the examples again and practise saying them.**

C 🔊 55 **Listen and write the last three words of each sentence.**

1 Our market share is increasing faster here *than in Korea*
2 The Hilton is bigger ....
3 Our main competitor offers a cheaper service ....
4 The rate of unemployment is worse ....
5 She's more popular ....

🔊 55 **Listen again and practise saying the sentences.**

STRESS AND INTONATION

D **Look at the example and explanation. Then underline the word which has a different stress pattern in each line (1–5).**

Example: popular — <u>expensive</u> — luxury

Explanation: We say POPular and LUXury (stress on the first syllable) but exPENsive (stress on the second syllable).

1 market — campaign — success
2 profitable — competitive — comfortable
3 quality — department — producer
4 thousand — million — event
5 marketing — attractive — company

🔊 56 **Listen and check your answers. Then listen again and practise saying the words.**

MEETINGS

A **Put the words in the correct order to make sentences often used in meetings.**

1 think / you're / I / right / .
I think you're right.

2 agree / I'm / I / afraid / don't / .

3 about / you / this / How / feel / do / ?

4 the / really / I / idea / like / .

5 about / sites / using / networking / How / social / ?

🔊 **57 Listen and check your answers. Then listen again and practise saying the sentences.**

B **Match the language functions (a–d) to the sentences in exercise A.**

a) Asking for an opinion [ ]   c) Disagreeing [ ]

b) Agreeing [1] [ ]   d) Making a suggestion [ ]

C **Number the opening sentences from a meeting in the correct order.**

a) Leo: Well, I think we should aim at sports enthusiasts, in all age groups. [ ]

b) Özgür: I suggest the middle and lower income groups. We have a quality product and we want it to be a bit cheaper than our competitors'. [ ]

c) Özgür: Hmm. I'm not sure about that. Teenagers don't find this kind of design attractive. [ ]

d) Ann: So let's start then. My first question is, what is our target market? [1]

e) Ann: Fine. That makes our work easier. And what income group? [ ]

f) Leo: You're probably right. Let's target men and women in the age group 25-plus, then. [ ]

LISTENING PRACTICE

D 🔊 **53 Listen and tick the best response, a), b) or c), for each question you hear.**

1 a) Yes. You are right.
  b) Well, I think sales are better than for other products.
  c) In airport and railway station shops. [ ]

2 a) I think we should target single men and women in the upper income group.
  b) Central Europe is the main target.
  c) Well, consumer behaviour is different here.

3 a) Not on TV or radio this time!
  b) We should advertise more.
  c) Let's start the campaign in August.

4 a) Our market share is very small.
  b) Yes, they are the market leader in that area.
  c) Well, the price isn't quite right.

5 a) Let's relaunch it under a different brand name.
  b) At the end of the summer holiday.
  c) I'm afraid I don't agree.

6 a) Yes. We should target middle-aged women.
  b) Yes. Let's do more market research next year.
  c) Sales always go down in winter.

SURVIVAL BUSINESS ENGLISH

SOUND WORK

A **Underline the silent letter in these words.**

ai<u>s</u>le	debt	island	salmon
answer	fasten	know	sandwich
autumn	foreign	lamb	talk
climb	half	receipt	Wednesday

🔊 **59 Listen and check your answers. Then listen again and practise saying the words.**

B 🔊 **60 Listen to the pronunciation of the word *are* in these sentences.**

1 We <u>are</u> looking for a bigger warehouse.
  /ə/

2 Five companies <u>are</u> competing for this contract.
   /ə/

3 Our profit figures <u>are</u> improving.
   /ər/

4 Many German companies <u>are</u> investing in Turkey.
    /ər/

> **Tips**
>
> 1 Notice that *are* is often pronounced /ə/ or /ər/.
> 2 *you're = you are*   *we're = we are*   *they're = they are*
>   • The meaning is the same.
>   • The contracted forms are not used in formal business correspondence.

🔊 **60 Listen to the examples again and practise saying them.**

Tips

I'm not = I am not
isn't = is not
aren't = are not
• The meaning is the same.
• The contracted forms are not used in formal business correspondence.

C 🔊 **61 Listen and complete the sentences.**

1 <u>You're   planning</u> new outlets in Boston and Miami, is that right?
2 ....'.................... setting up a subsidiary in Brazil.
3 What.. research into?
4 Our competitors................................ .... abroad.
5 What.. to achieve?
6 .... looking for new offices?

🔊 **61 Listen again and practise saying the sentences.**

D 🔊 **62 Listen to the pronunciation of the underlined words.**

1 We <u>aren't</u> looking for new markets.
2 They <u>aren't</u> competing for that contract.

3 Our turnover <u>isn't</u> increasing.
4 She <u>isn't</u> working tomorrow.

🔊 **62 Listen to the examples again and practise saying them.**

E 🔊 **63 Listen and complete the sentences. Use contracted forms.**

1 ......*They*...... ......*aren't*...... investing in Indonesia.

2 .... planning to start a new business.

3 .... attracting a lot of new customers.

4 .... growing very fast.

5 .... launching it until September.

TALKS AND PRESENTATIONS

A **Match the sentence halves.**

1 As you know, I'm here today
   to tell you
2 Firstly, I'd like to look at our
3 Good afternoon. I'd like to
   welcome you all
4 Hi, everyone. Good to see
5 My talk today is
6 What I'd like to do today is to

a) present our new products.
b) in three main parts.
c) performance over the last three
    months.
d) about our new project in Brazil.
e) you all. My name's Rita Horvath.
f) here this afternoon.

B **Match the language functions (a–c) to the sentences in exercise A.**

a) Greeting the audience   ☐   ☐
b) Introducing the topic   1   ☐
c) Giving a plan of the talk   ☐   ☐

LISTENING PRACTICE

C 🔊 **64 Read the questions (1–5). Then listen to the conversations and tick the best response, a, b or c, to each of the questions.**

1 What kind of building does the man's company want?
   a) A larger one.
   b) A cheaper one. ✓
   c) A smaller one.

2 What is the man's opinion of the February sales figures?
   a) They were better last month.
   b) They are better than in January.
   c) They aren't much better this month.

3 Which one of these statements is true?
   a) Tom and Chris are in Azerbaijan to set up a subsidiary.
   b) The woman doesn't know what she's talking about.
   c) Chris wants to negotiate a contract.

4 Which part of the woman's presentation will be about the features of the
   new product?
   a) The first.
   b) The second.
   c) The third.

5 What do the man and the woman agree about?
   a) Sales figures are going down.
   b) They need to work harder.
   c) The marketing strategy is not good.

UNIT **10** | # Communication

SOUND WORK

**INDIVIDUAL
SOUNDS**

A 🔊 65 **Listen to the difference between /v/ and /w/.**

/v/	/w/
video	**w**in
value	**w**ay

B 🔊 66 **Complete the sentences with the words you hear.**
1 Their ..website.. is .... exciting.
2 In my ...., it's a .... of money.
3 .... site do you .... most often?
4 The .... Wide Web is of great .... to advertisers.
5 If you .... to .... that site, you need a valid password.
6 I received a .... warning.

🔊 66 **Listen again and practise saying the sentences.**

**CONNECTED
SPEECH**

C 🔊 67 **Listen and tick the sentences you hear.**
1 a) We take the early flight. b) We'll take the early flight. ✔
2 a) They work hard. b) They'll work hard.
3 a) I do it for them. b) I'll do it for them.
4 a) You have to download it. b) You'll have to download it.
5 a) They buy the same software. b) They'll buy the same software.
6 a) We try all the search engines. b) We'll try all the search engines.

D 🔊 68 **Listen to the pronunciation of the contracted forms.**
1 **I'll** show you. 4 **She'll** buy them.
2 **You'll** need it. 5 **We'll** watch it.
3 **He'll** want one. 6 **They'll** do it.

🔊 68 **Listen to the examples again and practise saying them.**

**STRESS AND
INTONATION**

E 🔊 69 **Listen to the conversations. Notice how Speaker B uses stress to correct Speaker A.**
1 A: So the flight's boarding at gate thirty. 2 A: Right. So I can come any Tuesday.
  B: No, it's gate thir<u>teen</u> we want.   B: Sorry, no. I said any <u>Thursday</u>.

F **Look at the conversations. Underline the part that Speaker B will stress to correct Speaker A.**
1 A: ... and you said check-in is at nine o'clock.
  B: No, it's <u>eight</u> o'clock, I'm afraid.
2 A: ... so that's Janet G-R-A-Y.
  B: Sorry, no. G-R-E-Y. Mrs Janet Grey.

72

3 A: Excuse me. Is the presentation on the first floor?

B: No, it's on the third floor. You'd better take the lift.

4 A: ... and your e-mail address is Vermeulen@pe.org.

B: That's not quite right. It's B-E, as in Belgium.

5 A: Let me just read the postcode back to you: CM20 3GE.

B: No. It's CM20 3JE.

6 A: So the fax number of their Sofia office is 359 2 968 61 58.

B: ... 61 98.

🔊 **70 Listen and check your answers. Then listen again and practise Speaker B's replies.**

MAKING ARRANGEMENTS **A** 🔊 **71 Listen to ten extracts from conversations and decide what each speaker is doing.**

• Write one letter, (a–e), next to the number of the speaker.
• Use each letter twice.

Speaker 1: ....b...........	**a)** Asking
Speaker 2:	**b)** Agreeing
Speaker 3:	**c)** Declining
Speaker 4:	**d)** Suggesting a different time
Speaker 5:	**e)** Apologising
Speaker 6:	
Speaker 7:	
Speaker 8:	
Speaker 9:	
Speaker 10:	

LISTENING PRACTICE

B 🔊 **72 Read the questions (1–6). Then listen to the conversations and tick the best response, a, b or c, to each of the questions.**

1 When are they going to discuss the contract?
 a) On Monday.
 b) On Tuesday.
 c) On Wednesday. ✓

2 Why does the man sound disappointed?
 a) They just talked.
 b) People were worried.
 c) The woman wasn't there.

3 How is the man going to the airport?
 a) By metro.
 b) By car.
 c) By taxi.

4 What does the man want Sandra to do?
 a) Come to a meeting.
 b) Come back before 11.30.
 c) Phone him later.

5 Why is the man late?
 a) All flights were half an hour late.
 b) He waited a long time at baggage reclaim.
 c) The weather was bad.

6 Where and when are they going to meet?
 a) In the cafeteria at 9 o'clock.
 b) At the registration desk at 10 o'clock.
 c) In the cafeteria after the conference.

SURVIVAL BUSINESS ENGLISH

SOUND WORK

GROUPS OF CONSONANTS | **A**

Tip

Many English words have groups of two or three consonant sounds at the beginning, in the middle or at the end of words. Pronounce those consonant sounds clearly together, without adding any other sound before or between them.

🔊 **73 Listen and write the missing letters to complete the words.**

1 fir**st**	reque___	ho___
2 __aff	__ore	___ategy
3 __eak	__ace	__e____
4 __ar__	__o____	___i__
5 __or__	__iri__	__eciali___

🔊 **73 Listen again and practise saying the words. Pay attention to the groups of consonant sounds.**

CONNECTED SPEECH | **B**

🔊 **74 Listen and complete the sentences with *should* or *shouldn't*.**

1 In Finland, you ......*should*...... never arrive late for an appointment.

2 In many countries, you .... write on business cards.

3 You .... offer your hand to shake immediately.

4 In Germany, you .... use the person's title before the surname.

5 In most countries, you .... point your finger at the person you're talking to.

6 So, before you go to a new country, you .... do your homework!

🔊 **74 Listen again and practise saying the sentences.**

STRESS AND INTONATION | **C**

Put the words from the box into the correct column according to their stress pattern.

~~adapt~~ arrangement arrive document important offer popular silence

1 O o	2 o O	3 O o o	4 o O o
custom	abroad	cultural	appointment
/ə/	/ə/	/ə//ə/	/ə/ /ə/-
....	......*adapt*......	....	....
....	....	....	....

D

🔊 **75 Listen to the words in exercise C and underline the /ə/ sounds (see page 52) that you hear. Then check your answers.**

🔊 **75 Listen again and practise saying the words.**

Note

Remember, all the /ə/ sounds are in the unstressed syllables.

E

🔊 **76 Tick (✓) the offers and requests where the speaker sounds polite. Cross (✗) the ones where the speaker does not sound polite.**

1 Could I use your phone? ✓

2 Could I use your computer? ✗

3 Would you like a drink?

4 Would you like a sandwich?

5 Could you tell me the way?

6 Could you check these figures?

Check your answers.

F 🔊 **77 Listen to these polite offers and requests. Practise saying them.**

1 Would you like some coffee?

2 Could you spell that for me?

3 Could I use the meeting room?

4 Would you like a copy of the brochure?

5 Could you make the travel arrangements for me?

6 Could I borrow your dictionary?

CONVERSATIONS

A **Two managers are talking about a problem. Complete the conversation with the sentences (a–f).**

a) Explain to them *why* we changed the schedule.

b) Try to find out exactly what each one of them is unhappy about.

c) I'll try that.

d) They're complaining about our new work schedule.

e) But, unfortunately, they still don't agree with a lot of the changes.

f) ~~What kind of problems?~~

A: So you're saying there are problems in Sales. *f* ....[1]

B: Well, it's the representatives. ..... [2]

A: Do you know what the best thing to do is? ..... [3]

B: I think they understand the reasons. ..... [4]

A: Well, maybe you should talk to them one by one. ..... [5]

B: OK then. ..... [6]

🔊 **78 Listen to the conversation and check your answers.**

LISTENING PRACTICE

B 🔊 **79 Listen and tick the best response, a), b) or c), for each item you hear.**

1 a) I really don't know. You should ask Tina – she's worked in Vietnam before. ✓

b) That's right. I'll call everyone on Friday morning.

c) Of course! You should always telephone first.

2 a) Yes. The last meeting was late in the afternoon, too.

b) All right. Just let me know when the next one is.

c) Well, he doesn't enjoy the work here, I'm afraid.

3 a) That's right, yeah. Never write on a business card.

b) Yes. Always offer and receive things with your right hand.

c) Yes, please. And I'll give you mine.

4 a) Well, normally we have a holiday in the summer.

b) Much the same as here. Most people have a nine-to-five job.

c) No, not many people work from home.

5 a) Yes. People speak Portuguese in Brazil, you know.

b) Good idea. We need to communicate more.

c) Try the Internet. The Lonely Planet website, for example.

6 a) Most young people now drink Italian-style coffee.

b) No, thanks. Just some water.

c) Well, in the morning I usually have orange juice and cereal.

SOUND WORK

-ed ENDINGS

What's the rule?

If the infinitive of a regular verb ends in /t/ or /d/, the *-ed* of the past simple form and of the past participle is pronounced /ɪd/ and the verb gets an extra syllable.

A ◀))80 **Listen to how these verb forms are pronounced.**

work	(1 syllable)	worked	(1 syllable)
end	(1 syllable)	ended	(2 syllables)
finish	(2 syllables)	finished	(2 syllables)
create	(2 syllables)	created	(3 syllables)
advertise	(3 syllables)	advertised	(3 syllables)
motivate	(3 syllables)	motivated	(4 syllables)

B **Underline the forms which are one syllable longer than the infinitive. Then check your answers.**

1	plan	planned		7	invite	invited
2	wait	<u>waited</u>		8	reward	rewarded
3	cope	coped		9	organise	organised
4	train	trained		10	interrupt	interrupted
5	manage	managed		11	develop	developed
6	decide	decided		12	recommend	recommended

◀))81 **Now listen and practise saying the pairs of verb forms.**

INDIVIDUAL SOUNDS

C ◀))82 **Listen to the difference between /ɒ/ and /ɔː/.**

/ɒ/	/ɔː/
n**o**t sp**o**t	n**ough**t sp**or**t
t**o**p j**o**b	sh**or**t c**our**se

D **Underline all the letters that are pronounced /ɔː/ in these sentences. Check your answers.**

1 How often do you write reports?
2 What sorts of bosses have you had?
3 Our office staff don't wear uniforms.
4 Robert has taught abroad for four years.

◀))83 **Listen and practise saying the sentences.**

CONNECTED SPEECH

E ◀))84 **Listen and complete the sentences. Use contractions ('s, 've, hasn't or haven't).**

1 .....*She's*..... gained a lot of experience.
2 .... finished everything.
3 .... sent his CV.
4 .... invited her for an interview.
5 .... selected anyone yet.
6 .... interviewed everyone.

◀))84 **Listen again and practise saying the sentences.**

A JOB INTERVIEW

A **Complete the extract from a job interview with the sentences (a–g).**

a) Are there any questions you'd like to ask us?

b) ~~First of all, why do you want this job?~~

c) I don't think conflict is a bad thing.

d) In addition, I'm very motivated and ready for a challenge.

e) Then, I always communicate those aims to the team members.

f) What are your strengths as a team leader?

g) What sort of people do you work well with?

A: Well, let's start, then. ..b..¹

B: I think my excellent experience of project management can contribute to the success of the department. .....²

A: You've just mentioned project management. There are twelve people in the project team. .....³

B: I like to have clear aims to begin with. I think that's essential for a team leader. .....⁴ They all need to know exactly where they're going.

A: Right. And what do you do about conflict in a team?

B: There's always some conflict in teams. .....⁵ You have to listen to people and help them to solve problems together. I think I'm good at that.

A: .....⁶

B: Well, I like to work with motivated and reliable people. And I like people with a sense of humour – that's great.

A: .....⁷

B: I've read your company brochure, but I would like some details of the projects you've been involved in recently ...

LISTENING PRACTICE

B 🔊 **85** **Listen and tick the best response, a), b) or c), for each question you hear.**

1 a) Nothing. I enjoyed all of it.
  b) Yes, of course. Things like working to tight deadlines. ✓
  c) Well, I was Assistant Office Manager.

2 a) I saw the advertisement in *The Norwich Herald*.
  b) I've worked for Alfitel for three months and I'm really enjoying it.
  c) I think I have the right qualifications and experience and I need a challenge.

3 a) I didn't have an opportunity to use my leadership skills.
  b) No, I didn't. It was a very boring place.
  c) I'd like to be Project Manager.

4 a) Cycling, playing chess and I love classical music.
  b) Well, I don't like paperwork.
  c) I'm a good team worker and I work well under pressure.

5 a) I think people can learn a lot from each other.
  b) I can work one weekend every month.
  c) Yes, I have negotiated contracts with important clients.

6 a) Yes, you can contact me any day after 2.30.
  b) I have included their details in my CV.
  c) Yes, of course. I have informed both of them.

Answer key

LANGUAGE WORK

1 Introductions

Vocabulary

A

2 Russia
3 Sweden
4 Poland
5 Germany
6 Argentina

B

2 Japanese
3 French
4 Spanish
5 English
6 Greek

C

Across

1 British
6 Sweden
8 US
9 Japan
11 Korean

Down

1 Brazil
2 India
3 Swiss
4 Finnish
5 Germany
7 France
10 UK

D

2 Holland (the Netherlands)
3 Pakistan
4 the Czech Republic
5 Turkey
6 Senegal

E

2 Portuguese
3 Swiss
4 Taiwanese
5 Slovak
6 Thai

F

Group 1
Adjectives ending in -an

Country	Nationality
Chile	Chilean
Iran	Iranian

Group 2
Adjectives ending in -ish

Country	Nationality
Finland	Finnish
Scotland	Scottish

Group 3
Adjectives ending in -ese

Country	Nationality
Sudan	Sudanese
Vietnam	Vietnamese

Group 4
Adjectives ending in -i

Country	Nationality
Bahrain	Bahraini
Iraq	Iraqi

Language review

A

2 's (is)
3 are
4 's (is)
5 are
6 'm (am); 's (is)
7 are; is

B

2 Where are they from?
3 What's (What is) her name?
4 My office is in Paris, but I'm (I am) not French.
5 Mrs Lopez is a lawyer.
6 Alex and Rob are from Italy.

C

2 Are Isabel and Luis from Spain?
3 Are you a programmer?
4 Are you and Tom in Marketing?
5 Am I in room 16 tomorrow?

D

2 a   3 b   4 d   5 c

E

2 Yes, I am.
3 No, you aren't. (No, you're not.)
4 Yes, you are.
5 No, she isn't.
6 Yes, he is.
7 No, I'm not.
8 No, we aren't. (No, we're not.)

Writing

A

2 She is married with two children.
3 Lucas and Mirjana are interested in travel.
4 Is Wizz Air a Hungarian company?
5 How do you do. I'm Ana Kostic, from RTVS.
6 The sales manager is very busy today.
7 My best friend is Brazilian. He is from Porto Seguro.

B

2 Akemi's
3 company's
4 What's
5 It's; isn't
6 aren't; We're

C

2 Mrs Kimura is Japanese.
3 Is Nokia Danish?
4 Paul is married with two children.
5 This is George Ellis, from Marketing.
(Note: Names of departments are sometimes spelt without a capital letter, e.g., marketing, accounts, etc.)
6 Mr Brown's new boss is from London, Ontario.

D

2 is from Altheim
3 a sales manager
4 company sells
5 business is
6 do business

2 Work and leisure
Vocabulary
A

2 flexible hours
3 travel opportunities
4 expense account
5 sports facilities
6 company cars
7 parking facilities
8 job security

B

2 March
3 winter
4 February
5 Tuesday
6 autumn

C

2 in
3 on
4 in
5 at
6 in
7 at
8 on
9 on
10 in
11 at

D

2 My boss and I don't like watching football on TV.
3 My colleagues and I often go to the cinema on Saturdays.
4 I quite like reading, but I hate listening to the radio.
5 Our new secretary sometimes plays tennis at the weekend.
6 How often do you go abroad on holiday?

E

2 at
3 Ø
4 at
5 Ø
6 in
7 Ø
8 in
9 in
10 at

What's the rule?
We do **not** use at, in or on before next, this, every or last in a time phrase.

F

2 e 3 b 4 a 5 c 6 d 7 c 8 a 9 e 10 b

Language review
A

2 has
3 like
4 goes
5 arrives
6 check
7 has
8 works
9 spends
10 enjoy

B

2 Jameel sometimes goes to conferences abroad.
3 Rick isn't usually very busy on Mondays.
4 We are never at home in the evening.
5 Do you always go to work by train?
6 James does not often travel on business.
7 I usually stay at home at the weekend.
8 Why are some people always late for work?

C

2 How often does Sedef visit clients?
3 Darius works late twice a week.
4 In the evening, we usually watch TV/We usually watch TV in the evening.
5 They are never at home on Saturdays.
6 She makes a lot of telephone calls every day.

Writing
A

2 arrives
3 starts
4 discusses
5 has
6 enjoys
7 studies

B

2 She goes to the UK every year in March.
3 Paul sometimes reads *The Financial Times*.
4 They live in Amsterdam, but they aren't Dutch.
5 Their office is in Oxford Street.
6 As you know, I work for the European Commission.
7 The Polish representatives arrive at Heathrow at 7.30 a.m.
8 Louise and Bill are from the United States.
9 How often do you watch the BBC?

C

First name:	Raoul
Surname:	Gautier
Age:	24
Marital status:	Single/~~Married~~
Occupation:	PR Manager
Address:	47, Avenue Aristide Briand, Toulouse
Telephone number:	55 78 43 00

D

The correct order is b, e, d, a, c.

3 Problems
Vocabulary
A

2 missing
3 crashes
4 broken
5 working

B

2 d 3 f 4 e 5 a 6 g 7 c

C

2 ✓
3 ✓
4 My boss is great, and my colleagues are very nice.
5 I can't do it fast enough. I need some help.
6 Come to our country! The food is delicious and the people are very friendly.

D

2 a 3 e 4 c 5 b 6 g 7 j 8 f 9 h 10 i

E

2 c 3 c 4 a 5 b 6 b 7 c

Language review
A

3 She doesn't finish work late. / She finishes work early.
4 We often work at the weekend.
5 They don't sell office equipment.
6 I don't make a lot of phone calls.
7 He writes reports.

B

2 Jim doesn't get lots of e-mails.
3 Jim has regular breaks.
4 Kate and Ross attend a lot of meetings.
5 Kate and Ross don't often entertain foreign visitors.
6 Jim doesn't read *The Financial Times*.

C

1 Kate and Ross get lots of e-mails, but Jim doesn't.
2 Kate and Ross don't have regular breaks, but Jim does.
3 Jim doesn't attend a lot of meetings, but Kate and Ross do.
4 Jim often entertains foreign visitors, but Kate and Ross don't.
5 Kate and Ross read *The Financial Times*, but Jim doesn't.

D

2	any	5	any	8	some
3	a	6	any	9	any
4	a	7	any	10	some

Writing

A

2 Their company is having a problem with their cash flow.
3 Our order is delayed.
4 It does not work properly.
5 It is very efficient.
6 She does not have an assistant.

B

2 They pay a lot of rent for a small office in the city centre.
3 When does the meeting finish?
4 Bill has a large office, but he does not have a company car.
5 How many people do they employ?

C

2 She is always on time and she is very efficient.
3 The new machine is small but it is very heavy.
4 The report is very long but it is very easy to understand.
5 There are a lot of changes and staff are worried about their jobs.
6 Our office is small but it is in the city centre.

D

2 inform
3 problem
4 damaged
5 missing
6 send

E

1 The office is small and crowded. In addition, the air conditioning does not work.
2 The screen is small and the picture is not very good. In addition, there is no remote control.
3 The photocopier does not work and there is only one phone line. In addition, the receptionist is never on time.

4 Travel

Vocabulary

A

Across		Down	
1	luggage	2	gate
5	security	3	duty
6	packing	4	single
9	arrives	7	alarm
12	leave	8	fasten
		10	row
		11	seat

B

2 your luggage
3 to queue
4 at a platform

C

2	on	7	at
3	by	8	for
4	off; to	9	to; to
5	at; at	10	from; to
6	from; to		

D

2 a   3 e   4 b   5 d

E

2	get off; get on	4	arrive
3	miss	5	are delayed

Language review

A

can (ability)	*can* (permission)	*can* (what is possible)
2 Can you use the new photocopier? 3 Can she speak Russian? 7 Can you hear me now?	4 Can I use your computer for half an hour, please? 6 Excuse me. Can I open the window? 8 Can I just make a phone call, please?	1 Can we fly direct from Rome to Tashkent? 5 Where can I buy phone cards? 9 Can we go to the airport by underground?

B

c 5   d 6   e 8   f 4   g 7   h 2   i 3

C

2 There's (There is)
3 There aren't (There are not)
4 there's (there is)
5 There're (There are)
6 Is there
7 There aren't (There are not)
8 Is there
9 there are
10 there isn't (there is not)

D

2 there; It
3 It; there
4 It; it
5 There; it
6 it; it; there

Writing

A

2 I'd like to book a room <u>from</u> Sunday 5th to Thursday 9th of this month.
3 I'm ringing to <u>confirm</u> my flight details.
4 Would you <u>like</u> an aisle or a window seat?
5 Can we meet at the railway <u>station</u> at 8.30?
6 There <u>are</u> two restaurants where you can entertain business guests.

B

2 two nights
3 hotel
4 Please
5 costs
6 per night
7 booking
8 Thank

C

2 Ms (~~Mr~~)
3 single (~~double~~)
4 Tuesday (~~Thursday~~)
5 including full breakfast (~~breakfast not included~~)

5 Food and entertaining

Vocabulary

A

2 a 3 c 4 b 5 c 6 a 7 a 8 b 9 c 10 a

B

Across
4 sour
6 meat
8 soup
9 tuna

Down
2 tiramisu
3 pizza
4 salmon
5 fruit
7 tip

C

2 c 3 d 4 b 5 a 6 e

D

2 soup
3 salad
4 a receipt
5 a bill

Language review

A

Countable	Uncountable
credit card	beef
hamburger	fish[1]
restaurant	money
waiter	soup[2]

1 *Fish* is uncountable when it means 'a kind of food'; it is countable when it means 'an animal that lives in water'.
2 *Soup* is usually uncountable: *We eat a lot of soup in winter.* Sometimes, however, it can be countable, as in *They sell a wide range of tinned soups.*

B

	singular countable noun	plural countable noun	uncountable noun
+	1 I'd like a dessert.	4 I'd like some chips.	5 I'd like some soup.
–	3 I don't want a large glass.	8 There aren't any tables free.	9 We don't have any milk.
?	6 Is there a Chinese restaurant in town?	2 Are there any green apples?	7 Is there any meat in it?

C

2 many
3 many
4 much
5 many
6 many
7 much
8 much

D

2 d 3 b 4 a 5 c 6 f 7 e

Writing

A

2 minutes *not* minute
3 it *not* he
4 the *not* a
5 dishes *not* dish
6 meat *not* meet
7 book *not* booking

B

The correct order is b, a, f, e, c, d.

C

2 book
3 menu
4 vegetarian
5 confirm
6 again
7 Yours

6 Buying and selling

Vocabulary

A

2 a 3 b 4 b 5 c 6 a 7 a

B

Across
2 buyer
4 receipt
7 free
9 reward
10 benefits

Down
1 period
3 return
5 choose
6 credit
8 save

C

2 to e-mail
3 to pay
4 to promote
5 to say

D

2 e 3 f 4 d 5 a 6 c

E

2 retail
3 competitor
4 guarantee period
5 wholesale
6 after-sales service

Language review

A

2	were	6	was; were
3	were	7	were
4	was	8	were
5	were; were; was		

B

2	cost	5	give	8	spent
3	flew	6	paid	9	take
4	got	7	sell	10	wrote

C

2	wrote	5	paid
3	got	6	flew
4	spent		

D

2 introduced
3 went
4 reached
5 stayed
6 continued
7 increased
8 wanted
9 delayed
10 launched
11 went
12 was
13 grew
14 reached

E

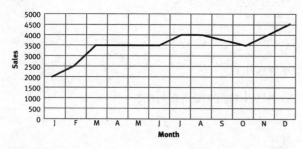

Writing

A

2 Before they place an order, a lot of people like to <u>ask</u> questions.
3 Please quote us <u>a</u> price for the goods listed below.
4 This special promotion is only <u>for</u> a short time.
5 Unfortunately, we wrote the wrong delivery <u>address</u> on the package.
6 We paid a €200 <u>deposit</u> and the rest in 12 monthly instalments.

B

2 launched *not* launch
3 sales *not* sale
4 experienced *not* experience
5 show *not* showing
6 They *not* The

7 People

Vocabulary

A

2	ambitious	5	sociable
3	hard-working	6	punctual
4	creative		

B

2	to	5	at	8	on
3	for	6	for	9	with
4	Ø	7	with	10	Ø

C

2 f   3 e   4 b   5 g   6 a   7 d   8 c

Language review

A

1	began	6	found
2	bring	7	went
3	caught	8	knew
4	came	9	leave
5	drive	10	sent

B

2	drive; caught	7	come (*or* go)
3	leave	8	find
4	send; bring	9	catch
5	begin	10	go
6	knew		

C

b 4   c 10   d 8   e 9   f 5   g 1   h 3   i 7   j 2

D

2 Did he like to work in a team?
3 Were they hard-working?
4 Was Mrs Whitehead popular with her colleagues?
5 Did she know how to motivate people?
6 Were you happy to work with Sandra?

E

b 4   c 5   d 2   e 6   f 3

F

2 No, we didn't.
3 Yes, they did.
4 No, they weren't.
5 No, she doesn't.
6 Yes, it was.
7 Yes, they were.
8 Yes, I can.

G

Sample questions
2 Where did her parents move to?
3 Was she a successful student? / Was she born in Aarhus? / Was she good with numbers?
4 What were her favourite subjects?
5 Where did her father work?
6 Did the students like her book?
7 Where did she do an MBA?
8 What did she do at the age of 25?
9 Is Nielsen Electronics successful?
10 How many countries does it have branches in?

Writing

A

2 so	5 because
3 but	6 so
4 because	7 but; because

B

3 is	6 any
4 the	7 a
5 ✓	8 of

C

2 g   3 a   4 d   5 e   6 c   7 b

8 Advertising

Vocabulary

A

Across	Down
1 launch	1 luxury
4 export	2 slogans
7 aim	3 hoarding
8 flyer	5 time
10 Mass	6 home
12 niche	9 logo
13 agency	11 sample
14 word	13 ad
15 jingle	

Language review

A

2 larger	8 happier
3 easier	9 earlier
4 hotter	10 quieter
5 younger	11 thinner
6 newer	12 noisier
7 bigger	

B

2 more expensive
3 more competitive
4 worse
5 bigger
6 better
7 earlier
8 younger

C

2 more	7 a
3 difficult	8 easier
4 the	9 worse
5 most	10 less
6 than	

D

2 a   3 g   4 b   5 f   6 d   7 c

E

Sample answers
2 a little (or a bit)
3 a little (or a bit) bigger
4 a lot (or much) fewer
5 much (or a lot) more expensive than
6 is much (or a lot) lighter than

Writing

A

2 interested in
3 please confirm
4 like to know
5 look forward to

B

The correct order is f, d, c, e, b, a, g

C

To:	Tom
From:	Kim
Subject:	Impex account

Hi Tom,

Mr Stankov from Impex contacted me this morning. He is very unhappy because he hasn't received the samples of our new products. He says he may not order from us again.

Could you please send him another box of samples as soon as possible. You know Russia is a very important market for us and we don't want to lose this customer.

Many thanks for dealing with this.

Best regards,

Kim

9 Companies

Vocabulary

A

2 manufactures
3 provided
4 has
5 exports
6 launched

B

2 c   3 d   4 e   5 a

C

2 supplies
3 employs
4 sell abroad
5 introduced

D

2 d   3 b   4 f   5 c   6 a

Language review

A

2 developing	8 listening
3 increasing	9 referring
4 running	10 manufacturing
5 staying	11 working
6 getting	12 happening
7 taking	

B

2 We are sorry to hear the new machines <u>are</u> not working very well.

3 Many foreign companies <u>are</u> investing in Turkey.

4 <u>Are</u> Sonara's sales figures improving?

5 We <u>are</u> (or 're) looking for a manager with a lot of experience in finance.

6 <u>Is</u> Wilhelm still checking the company accounts?

7 Unfortunately, the south of the country <u>is</u> not attracting many investors.

8 You <u>are</u> (or 're) planning to break into the Brazilian market, aren't you?

C

2 is (she) working
3 are doing
4 are not (or aren't) increasing
5 is not (or isn't) planning
6 is dealing

D

2 Yes, they are.   6 No, I'm not.
3 No, they aren't.   7 Yes, she is.
4 No, he isn't.   8 No, it isn't.
5 Yes, we are.

E

2 are improving; improve
3 takes; is taking
4 organises; 's (or is) organising
5 test; 's (or is) testing
6 're (or are) using; use

F

2 answer   7 is speaking
3 are thinking   8 are employing
4 speaks   9 is answering
5 does (the company) employ   10 translate
6 think

Writing

A

3 says *not* say   7 ✓
4 do *not* doing   8 brands *not* brand
5 ✓   9 it also *not* its also
6 wear *not* wearing   10 ✓

B

Dear Sir or Madam,
We are writing to request further information about your new range of trainers.
We are a large chain of retailers of sportswear. We are looking for a manufacturer of footwear for the French market.
We operate from over 400 stores and always order in large quantities. Could you please send us details of special discounts for such orders and your latest catalogue.
We look forward to hearing from you.
Yours faithfully,
Barbara Costa

C

2 but also   5 The second one
3 For example   6 as well as
4 The first one   7 Finally

10 Communication

Vocabulary

A

Across
1 briefing
3 join
5 mail
8 access
10 wiki
11 check
13 SMS
14 post

Down
1 blog
2 calls
4 notice
6 face
7 swaps
9 social
12 Chat

B

2 at   9 for
3 at   10 on
4 to   11 until (or till)
5 in   12 in
6 From   13 by
7 to   14 of
8 for

Language review

A

2 'm going to put
3 're going to expand
4 Is (he) going to talk
5 isn't going to meet
6 's going to call
7 're going to complain

B

2 e   3 f   4 a   5 d   6 b

C

2 won't   7 won't
3 'll   8 will
4 will   9 'll
5 won't   10 will
6 won't

D

2 'My computer's not working properly.' 'Don't worry. I'<u>ll</u> (or will) call our IT specialist.'

3 Our visitors from Korea <u>are</u> arriving next Thursday at 11.30.

4 We can't be sure that people <u>will</u> have more free time in 20 years' time.

5 Are you going <u>to</u> apply for the post of Systems Analyst with GBS Electronics?

6 Do you think you'<u>ll</u> (or will) be able to come to the conference?

7 I can't make it tomorrow morning, I'm afraid. I'<u>m</u> (or am) giving a talk at the trade fair.

8 It'<u>ll</u> (or will) cost too much to employ an extra IT assistant.

9 We are certain Internet security <u>is</u> going to get better.

10 I'<u>ll</u> (or will) have the report on your desk before Friday, I promise.

Writing

A

2 He won't catch the earlier flight.
3 He won't check in until 8.45.
4 He hopes there won't be a delay.
5 Judith will book him on a later flight.
6 She won't book him on the early morning flight.
7 Dave arrives at 10.50 so he won't be late for the meeting.

B

2 d   3 e   4 f   5 c   6 a

C

2 leaving
3 I should
4 Please
5 later
6 Sorry
7 early
8 arriving
9 delay
10 you'll

D

Sample answer

To:	travelsection@jeffreys.co.uk
From:	Dave.Walton@jeffreys.be
Subject:	Travel arrangements

Hi Judith,

THX for looking into this.

PLS book me on the 9.45 flight if that's no problem.

Those flights are usually on time and they always arrange for someone to pick me up at the airport, so I should be fine.

THX again.

Best,

Dave

11 Cultures

Vocabulary

A

2 a   3 c   4 b   5 a   6 b   7 c   8 c   9 b

B

2 shift
3 part
4 public holiday
5 childcare
6 time off
7 title
8 language

C

2 performance
3 customer
4 control
5 trust

Language review

A

2 c   3 h   4 d   5 a   6 e   7 b   8 g

B

2 shouldn't
3 shouldn't
4 should
5 should
6 shouldn't
7 should
8 should

C

2 should
3 shouldn't
4 should
5 should
6 shouldn't
7 shouldn't
8 should
9 shouldn't

D

2 Would you
3 Would you
4 Could I
5 Could you
6 Could you; Would you

Writing

A

2 but
3 because
4 so
5 but
6 because
7 so
8 and

B

Sample answer

Dear Ms Roberts,

I enjoy working in Accounts. My colleagues are great and the work is often challenging.

Unfortunately, I have problems with some of the recent changes. I would like my hours of work to be more flexible because of my family situation.

I also have to spend too much time writing reports.

Finally, in the past there was much more face-to-face communication in the company, and that was very good.

I would like to see you to talk about all this in more detail. Could you please let me know when is a good time for you.

Best wishes,

Marco Albu

C

2 c   3 d   4 e   5 a

D

b 3   c 5   d 1   e 4

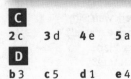

12 Jobs

Vocabulary

A

2 a   3 c   4 b   5 b   6 a   7 a   8 b   9 c
10 b   11 c   12 b

B

2 in   5 for
3 in   6 as
4 for   7 in *or* for

Language review

A

2 Have Khalid and Lucien changed jobs frequently?
3 Has Natalia had several jobs since leaving university?
4 Have Laura and Stella both applied for the same job?
5 Have you and Tim ever had difficulties getting along with Mr Dumas?
6 Have you ever worked in Central Asia?

B

b 1   c 6   d 3   e 4   f 5

C

2 Yes, they have.
3 Yes, I (*or* we) have.
4 No, they haven't.
5 No, I (*or* we) haven't.
6 Well, Luis has, but I'm afraid I haven't.

D

1 The last time I saw her was three months ago / last week / at 9 o'clock / yesterday morning / in 2007 / five minutes ago.
2 They haven't been very successful this year / for the past ten days / so far / over the last five years.

E

2 've received (have received)
3 phoned
4 have you selected
5 started
6 arrived
7 haven't finished
8 've already selected (have already selected)
9 Have you invited
10 thought
11 've finished (have finished)
12 didn't have

Writing

A

2 What are your strengths?
3 What do you do in your free time?
4 What kind of people do you work well with?
5 What has been your greatest achievement?
6 What did you like about your last job?
7 What do you want to do in the future?

B

Sample answers

1 I speak German and Italian and I'm learning Japanese.
2 I'm a very organised person and I get on well with people.
3 I go swimming every weekend and I sometimes play tennis.
4 I like to work with reliable people and I also like people who have a sense of humour.
5 I did really well on my MBA course and I'm quite proud of that.
6 My colleagues were very helpful and the atmosphere in our department was great.
7 I expect my job to give me fresh challenges because I want to keep learning and to give the best of myself.

C

2 a   3 e   4 g   5 b   6 f   7 c

TALK BUSINESS

Introduction

Vowels		
/ɒ/	/e/	/ɑː/
1 job	1 sell	1 card
2 knowledge	2 friendship	2 heart
3 want	3 said	3 laugh
/eɪ/	/eə/	/aɪ/
1 pay	1 share	1 price
2 break	2 chair	2 buyer
3 train	3 their	3 height
Consonants		
/ʃ/	/s/	/j/
1 option	1 sell	1 year
2 conscious	2 advice	2 Europe
3 insurance	3 scientific	3 million

1 Introductions

Sound work

A

3 ✓   4 ✓   5 ✗   6 ✓   7 ✓

D *See audio script 5.*

F *See audio script 7.*

Survival business English

A

2 f   3 a   4 h   5 g   6 i   7 d   8 j   9 e   10 b

B *See audio script 8.*

C

2 a   3 b   4 c   5 a   6 b   7 c   8 a

2 Work and leisure

Sound work

B *See audio script 11.*

D

2	discusses	3
3	starts	1
4	closes	2
5	delivers	3
6	visits	2
7	changes	2
8	completes	2

F *See audio script 15.*

Survival business English

A

2 f   **3** b   **4** a   **5** d   **6** e

B

2 b   **3** b   **4** c   **5** a   **6** c   **7** a   **8** b   **9** a   **10** c

3 Problems

Sound work

B *See audio script 18.*

C

In these words, the second letter *a* is pronounced /ɪ/ as in quick fix.

E *See audio script 21.*

G *See audio script 23.*

Survival business English

A *See audio script 24.*

B

The correct order is b, f, d, i, h, c, e, g, a.

C

2 c   **3** b   **4** c   **5** a   **6** c

4 Travel

Sound work

B *See audio script 28.*

C *See audio script 28.*

D

3 –   **4** +   **5** –   **6** +   **7** +   **8** –

E *See audio script 30.*

Survival business English

A *See audio script 31.*

B *See audio script 32.*

C

2 a   **3** c   **4** c   **5** a   **6** b   **7** b   **8** b   **9** a   **10** c

5 Food and entertaining

Sound work

B *See audio script 35.*

C *See audio script 36.*

D

1 reCEIPT (but: SERvice; MEnu)
2 deSSERT (but: SAlad; STARter
3 AUbergine (but: mouSSAka; toMAto)
4 deLIcious (but: POpular; Average)
5 eQUIPment (but: QUAlity; CUStomer)

Survival business English

A *See audio script 38.*

B

b 7   **c** 4   **d** 6   **e** 2   **f** 1   **g** 8   **h** 5

C

2 b   **3** a   **4** b   **5** c   **6** a

6 Buying and selling

Sound work

A

2 d   **3** e   **4** a   **5** b   **6** g   **7** f

B *See audio script 42.*

C *See audio script 43.*

Survival business English

A *See audio script 44.*

B

2 a   **3** b   **4** c   **5** b   **6** c   **7** a   **8** c

7 People

Sound work

A *See audio script 46.*

C *See audio script 48.*

D *See audio script 49.*

Survival business English

A

2	too	**5**	suggestion
3	down	**6**	leave
4	manage		

B

b 1   **c** 2   **d** 5   **e** 6   **f** 3

C

Speaker 1: b	Speaker 5: a
Speaker 2: d	Speaker 6: d
Speaker 3: c	Speaker 7: a
Speaker 4: b	Speaker 8: c

D

2 a   **3** c   **4** b   **5** b   **6** a

8 Advertising

Sound work

C *See audio script 55.*

D

1 MARket (but: camPAIGN; sucCESS)
2 comPEtitive (but: PROfitable; COMfortable)
3 QUAlity (but: dePARTment; proDUcer)
4 eVENT (but: THOUsand; MILlion)
5 aTTRACtive (but: MARketing; COMpany)

Survival business English

A *See audio script 57.*

B

a 3　　b 1, 4　　c 2　　d 5

C

The correct order is d, a, c, f, e, b.

D

2 a　　3 a　　4 c　　5 b　　6 b

9 Companies

Sound work

A *See audio script 59.*

C *See audio script 61.*

E *See audio script 63.*

Survival business English

A

2 c　　3 f　　4 e　　5 b　　6 a

B

a 3, 4　　b 1, 6　　c 2, 5

C

2 b　　3 c　　4 b　　5 a

10 Communication

Sound work

B *See audio script 66.*

C *See audio script 67.*

F *See audio script 70.*

Survival business English

A

Speaker 2: a　　Speaker 7: e
Speaker 3: b　　Speaker 8: c
Speaker 4: e　　Speaker 9: d
Speaker 5: d　　Speaker 10: a
Speaker 6: c

B

2 a　　3 b　　4 c　　5 b　　6 a

11 Cultures

Sound work

A *See audio script 73.*

B *See audio script 74.*

C *See audio script 75.*

D *See audio script 75.*

E

3 ✓　　4 ✗　　5 ✓　　6 ✗

Survival business English

A

2 d　　3 a　　4 e　　5 b　　6 c

B

2 c　　3 b　　4 b　　5 c　　6 a

12 Jobs

Sound work

B *See audio script 81.*

D *See audio script 83.*

E *See audio script 84.*

Survival business English

A

2 d　　3 f　　4 e　　5 c　　6 g　　7 a

B

2 c　　3 a　　4 c　　5 a　　6 c

Audio scripts

Introduction

1

The sounds of English
Vowel sounds

/ɪ/	quick fix
/iː/	clean sheet
/e/	sell well
/æ/	bad bank
/ɑː/	smart card
/ɒ/	top job
/ɔː/	short course
/ʊ/	good books
/uː/	school rules
/ʌ/	much luck
/ɜː/	first term
/ə/	a'bout 'Canada

Diphthongs

/eɪ/	play safe
/aɪ/	my price
/ɔɪ/	choice oil
/aʊ/	downtown
/əʊ/	go slow
/ɪə/	near here
/eə/	fair share

Consonants

1 Contrasting voiceless and voiced consonants

Voiceless		Voiced	
/p/	pay	/b/	buy
/f/	file	/v/	value
/t/	tax	/d/	deal
/θ/	think	/ð/	this
/tʃ/	cheap	/dʒ/	job
/s/	sell	/z/	zero
/k/	card	/g/	gain
/ʃ/	option	/ʒ/	decision

2 Other consonants

/m/	mine
/n/	net
/ŋ/	branding
/h/	high
/l/	loss
/r/	rise
/w/	win
/j/	year

2
1 German; Turkish
2 France; Japan
3 Poland; Oman
4 Swedish; Greek
5 Russian; Kuwaiti
6 England; Italy
7 Brazilian; American

3
France; French
Spain; Spanish
Denmark; Danish
Wales; Welsh

4
an engineer; She's an engineer.
a sales assistant; He's a sales assistant in a supermarket.

5
1 Azim is an Uzbek airline pilot.
2 Jameel, meet Eric. He's in Accounts.
3 Anita has a lot of interests outside work.
4 This is Olga. She works for us in Odessa.
5 Liz works as a chemist for an Irish company.

6
Bra•zil; Bra•zil•ian
Chi•na; Chi•nese

7
1 She's from A•mer•i•ca/She's A•mer•i•can.
2 He's from It•al•y/He's I•tal•ian.
3 They're from Brit•ain/They're Brit•ish.
4 I'm from Ja•pan/I'm Jap•a•nese.
5 We're from Can•a•da/ We're Ca•na•di•an.
6 It's from Pol•and/It's Pol•ish.
7 So you're from Hun•gar•y/So you're Hun•gar•i•an.

8
A: Hello. My name's Francis – Francis Wells. I'm the new accountant.
B: Hi! I'm Tom Murphy. Nice to meet you, Francis.
A: Pleased to meet you, Tom. Are you in Accounts, too?
B: No, I'm not. I'm in Sales. I'm Assistant Sales Manager.
A: Mm, that's interesting. And how's business?
B: Not too bad.

9
1 Is he an accountant?
2 Are you with Nokia?
3 Are you French?
4 Are you married?
5 Is she the new sales assistant?
6 Are they all from Japan?
7 Would you like a coffee?
8 Is Kauf a German company?

10
sit; site; fill; file

11
/ɪ/ as in quick fix: Swiss; business; office; dinner
/aɪ/ as in my price: client; cycling; design; arrive

12
likes; works
opens; watches
telephones; finishes

13
1 travels
2 discusses
3 starts
4 closes
5 delivers
6 visits
7 changes
8 completes

14
a large office; in a large office; He works in a large office

15
1 He works until eight o'clock.
2 He's interested in advertising.
3 She gets up at six and does exercises.
4 She does a lot of overtime.
5 He has a lot of meetings in the afternoon.

16
1 a) A magazine, sometimes.
  b) No, but I write a lot of letters.
  c) About once a month.
2 a) Well, I usually arrive at 8.30.
  b) I go to Geneva twice a year.
  c) Yes, I work a lot every day.
3 a) I usually arrive early.
  b) Around 4.30.
  c) Sometimes, in summer.
4 a) Yes, but I don't like answering the phone.
  b) In the morning. It's very quiet.
  c) My colleagues. They're just fantastic!
5 a) It's really good at the moment.
  b) With Japan and sometimes with Russia
  c) €20,000.
6 a) 'I think it's one of the Baltic states.
  b) No, I work for Siemens.
  c) No, but I live and work in Tallinn.
7 a) I'm really keen on football and jogging.
  b) Yes. Of course I do.
  c) Well, I don't enjoy doing overtime.
8 a) Every day, but not on Fridays.
  b) 35, but I often do overtime.
  c) Yes. I really enjoy having flexible hours.
9 a) Once a week, on Friday mornings.
  b) Meetings usually start at 9 o'clock.
  c) Well, I always enjoy meeting new people.
10 a) Yes. I want to work for an international company.
  b) I'm always busy on Wednesdays.
  c) Good people to work with and enough money to live on!

17
late; want; carry; can't

18
1 dangerous
2 space
3 great
4 quality
5 watch
6 soft
7 travel
8 bag
9 narrow
10 hard
11 part
12 fast

19
manager; package; damaged

20
Do you live in a city?
Do you go to meetings?
How often do you travel abroad?
What do you do?

21
1 Do you drive to work?
2 What time do you start work?
3 When do you finish work?
4 Who do you report to?
5 Why do you do so much overtime?

22
Do you work in an office?
Do you travel a lot?

23
Do you work in August?
Do you socialise with colleagues?
Do you like your job?

24
1 I think there's something wrong with their telephone. The line is engaged all the time.
2 The coffee machine is broken. Let's get a new one.
3 We'll have to walk, I'm afraid. The lift is out of order.
4 I can't do the photocopying. There isn't any A4 paper. Where can I get some?
5 There's a problem with the invoice. The figures are wrong.
6 There are no instructions in the package and one piece is missing.

25
Belco: Good morning. Belco Electronics. How can I help you?
Steve: Good morning. Steve Jenkins here. Well, it's about the Max 3000 computer software. I'm afraid there are no instructions in the box.
Belco: Oh, I'm very sorry to hear that. It's the Max 3000 you bought yesterday, is it?
Steve: Yes, that's right.
Belco: Well, Mr Jenkins, just give me your address and I'll send you the instructions.
Steve: It's Flat 3, 18 Duke Road.
Belco: Right. I've got that. I'll put an instruction manual in the post for you straight away. And once again, sorry about our mistake.
Steve: Thank you very much. Goodbye.
Belco: Goodbye.

26
1 Could I speak to Mr Pinto, please?
2 I'm phoning about the new air conditioner. It doesn't work.
3 I'm afraid my invoice is wrong.
4 You're a bit late this morning.
5 Why don't they come to work on time?
6 Good morning, Sunrise Electronics. Ana Schwarz speaking.

27
airport; collect; home; money; office

28
/ə/ as in **a**bout Can**a**da: **co**llect; **co**nfirm
/əʊ/ as in **go** slow: **ho**me; **ho**tel
/ɒ/ as in t**o**p j**o**b: **o**ffice; sh**o**p
/ɔ:/ as in sh**or**t c**our**se: airp**or**t; passp**or**t
/ʌ/ as in m**u**ch l**u**ck: m**o**ney; **co**me

29
1 You can come.
2 They can't go.
3 He can't drive.
4 We can try.
5 She can't type.
6 I can wait.
7 She can pay.
8 You can't choose.

30
1 Can I use the phone, please?
2 Can I have a receipt, please?
3 Can I have the bill, please?
4 Can I have a glass of water, please?
5 Can I take one of these brochures, please?
6 Can I have an alarm call at 6.15, please?

31
1 A: So the first name is spelt F-R-A-N-C-I-S.
  B: No. It's F-R-A-N-C-E-S.
2 A: And the phone number is 3228 5959.
  B: Sorry, no. It's 3228 5859.
3 A: Ms Salgado's flight number is IP3208.
  B: Can you check that again, please? The number I have here is IB3208.

32
1 A: So you need two single rooms for three nights, from the twenty-third of this month?
  B: No. We need them from the twenty-first.
2 A: Right. One double room with a shower for two nights.
  B: Sorry. I'd like one with a bath, if possible.
3 A: ... and an aisle seat for Ms Sandra Davis. D-A-V-I-S ...
  B: Sorry, no. D-A-V-I-E-S
4 A: The train leaves from platform eighteen, is that right?
  B: No sir. You want platform sixteen for Newcastle.
5 A: Is the fitness centre on the ground floor?
  B: No, madam. It's on the fourth floor.
6 A: Let me just write this down ... Two hundred and fifty euros, and ...
  B: Sorry, no. That's two hundred and thirty euros.

33
1 a) Platform 5.
  b) At 6.30, if it's not delayed.
  c) Yes, and sometimes by plane.
2 a) Of course. You can just sit on the balcony and enjoy the view.
  b) Yes, there's CNN and BBC in each room.
  c) Every room has a computer, sir.
3 a) Yes. All flights are delayed.
  b) It's 020 7864 3400.
  c) Of course. Go ahead.
4 a) You can take a taxi or the airport minibus.
  b) You can make a reservation today.
  c) Only half an hour by bus.
5 a) Yes. There's a Lufthansa flight at 9.10.
  b) Single or return?
  c) No, I'm afraid you need to change at Toronto.
6 a) Yes. It opens at 7.30.
  b) Yes, we do. A single or a double?

c) No, but their fitness centre is great.
7 a) Yes, of course. Would you like an aisle or a window seat?
  b) Sure. What's the name of the company, sir?
  c) Yes. That's €35, please.
8 a) It arrives at 15.20.
  b) It's G3 1748.
  c) From gate 26.
9 a) What's your room number?
  b) I'm afraid that's too late.
  c) That's right. From platform 5.
10 a) The 3.30 flight to Qatar is now boarding.
  b) That's row 22, seat F.
  c) From terminal 2.

34
Tim; team
sit; seat

35
/ɪ/ as in qu**i**ck f**i**x: b**i**ll; b**u**siness; ch**i**cken; man**a**ger
/i:/ as in cl**ean** sh**eet**: m**ea**l; rec**ei**pt; Sw**e**den; sw**ee**t

36
1 It's for you.
2 How about some dessert?
3 Why don't we invite them for dinner?
4 Would you like some more juice?
5 How much time do you have for lunch?
6 There aren't a lot of restaurants in this area.
7 What do you recommend for the main course?
8 They have a lot of fish dishes on the menu.

37
1 service; receipt; menu
2 dessert; salad; starter
3 moussaka; aubergine; tomato
4 popular; average; delicious
5 equipment; quality; customer

38
1 Do you like Italian food?
2 Shall I ask for a menu in English?
3 Are you ready to order?
4 What would you like for the main course?
5 How's your food?
6 Now, Bob, how about a dessert?
7 Would you like to have coffee or tea?
8 Right. Shall we get the bill?

39
1 Dieter: Do you like Italian food?
  Bob: Oh yes, I love it.
2 Dieter: Shall I ask for a menu in English?
  Bob: No, that's all right, thanks. I need to practise my German a bit.
3 Dieter: Are you ready to order?
  Bob: I think I need a few more minutes.
4 Dieter: What would you like for the main course?
  Bob: Mm. Some lasagne would be nice.
5 Dieter: How's your food?
  Bob: Very nice, thank you. We must come here again next time I'm in Frankfurt.
6 Dieter: Now, Bob, how about a dessert?
  Bob: No, thanks. I don't really like sweet things.
7 Dieter: Would you like to have coffee or tea?
  Bob: Mm, yeah. I'd love an espresso, actually.
8 Dieter: Right. Shall we get the bill?
  Bob: Yes, let's. It's getting late.

40
1 Is that enough soup for you?
2 More rice?
3 What would you like to drink?
4 Would you like some more salmon?
5 Could you pass the salt, please?
6 Would you like some more?

41
1 gr**ew**; kn**ew**
2 **bough**t; **caugh**t
3 g**ave**; p**aid**
4 g**ot**; c**ost**
5 s**aid**; m**et**
6 s**old**; wr**ote**
7 t**ook**; p**ut**

42
1 Delivery's free.
2 There was no extra cost.
3 How much are they?
4 It was a great deal.
5 They're at the office.
6 We were away on business.
7 These models are easy to use.
8 The design's interesting.
9 We're looking for experienced sales reps.
10 They were on time.

43
1 talked; launched; stopped; worked
2 started; finished; needed; offered
3 increased; advised; improved; received
4 invited; expanded; exported; promoted

44
1 The Tex23 is our most popular laptop computer bag. It's designed for the business traveller and it's available in black or dark brown leather.
2 LockIt is an excellent protection against car crime. It's made of steel and is very strong.
3 With our new Medico testing kit, busy executives get useful and reliable information about their health. It's easy to use because it's fully automatic and it's so small you can carry it in your briefcase.
4 The Dual EM mobile phone is in the low price range, but it has a lot of special features. For example, you can read and write e-mail messages anywhere in the world.
5 Made for busy office people, the Exex desk chair is stylish and very well designed. Exex is the solution to your back problems.
6 With the Storage Wizard you can find any of your CDs or CD-ROMs quickly and easily. It's a very practical storage system that saves a lot of space and a lot of time.

45
1 Do you give a guarantee?
2 Do you have these goods in stock?
3 Could we pay in instalments?
4 What colours is this model available in?
5 Does it have any special features?
6 How expensive are they?
7 What's the target market?
8 What about delivery?

46
1 spend; spread; spring
2 staff; stress; strong
3 skill; screen; script
4 practical; problem; practise
5 helpful; punctual
6 increase; expand

47
an_office; in_an_office; He works_in_an_office.

48
1 I met_Ivan_in_August.
2 I didn't send_it_out_on time.
3 It wasn't_a good_idea to sell_it.
4 He had_a lot_of_interesting_ideas.
5 Yasmin gets_on well with_all_of_us.

49
1 A: Was Philip a good colleague?
  B: Yes, he was.
2 A: Did Barbara leave the company?
  B: No, she didn't.
3 A: Were they experienced?
  B: Yes, they were.
4 A: Did you do a lot of research?
  B: No, we didn't.
5 A: Was it a successful year for the company?
  B: No, it wasn't.
6 A: Did he often work late?
  B: Yes, he did.

50
1 How did you get to the office?
2 Where did she start her journey?
3 When did they found the company?
4 How old were they?
5 How far was it?

51
Speaker 1: All right, then. I'll think about it and get back to you by the end of the week.
Speaker 2: Let me tell you why they are thinking of leaving the company – no job security; unpaid overtime and only ten days annual leave – that's why!
Speaker 3: We could, for example, move Marko to a different department.
Speaker 4: I understand what you're saying, but we can't hire any more staff this year.
Speaker 5: There's too much work in Admin. Three people are trying to do the work of ten.
Speaker 6: If so many employees are unhappy, it's partly because we don't have a proper cafeteria and partly because we don't have any parking facilities whatsoever.
Speaker 7: We don't offer enough opportunities for promotion. We simply don't think enough about all the brilliant, ambitious employees that we have.
Speaker 8: Why don't we hire some part-time staff?

52
1 **a)** He never helped anyone.
  b) Yes, it was hard work.
  c) Because I didn't like my colleagues.
2 **a)** What kind of help do you need?
  b) Sorry, but everybody says I can do a great job.
  c) Thanks. I need a lot of support, too.
3 **a)** No, but he is very helpful.
  b) The problem is, business is bad.
  c) Well, he's rude sometimes.
4 **a)** I think there's a meeting.
  b) They just have too much work.
  c) Just a headache. I'll be better tomorrow.
5 **a)** Yes. My assistant has a lot of work, too.
  b) OK. What about a part-time one?
  c) Fine, but why did he leave the company?
6 **a)** Right. Let's try and solve this problem together.
  b) Well, they want to get to the top as fast as they can.
  c) I work long hours every day.

53
pro•mote   a•ttract•ive   qual•it•y
suc•cess   con•sum•er   hol•i•day

54
1 better; better than; It's better than last month.
2 cheaper; cheaper than; Life is cheaper here than in Paris.
3 heavier; heavier than; This model is heavier than the RT100.

55
1 Our market share is increasing faster here than in Korea.
2 The Hilton is bigger than the Palace.
3 Our main competitor offers a cheaper service than we do.
4 The rate of unemployment is worse than last year's.
5 She's more popular than our manager.

56
1 market; campaign; success
2 profitable; competitive; comfortable
3 quality; department; producer
4 thousand; million; event
5 marketing; attractive; company

57
1 I think you're right.
2 I'm afraid I don't agree.
3 How do you feel about this?
4 I really like the idea.
5 How about using social networking sites?

58
1 Where should we sell our new product?
2 Now then. What kind of person is our target consumer?
3 Where should we advertise?
4 Why is our new product losing market share?
5 In your opinion, when is a good time to relaunch our product?
6 Should we do some more market research?

59
aisle; answer; autumn; climb;
debt; fasten; foreign; half;
island; know; lamb; receipt;
salmon; sandwich; talk; Wednesday

60
1 We are looking for a bigger warehouse.
2 Five companies are competing for this contract.
3 Our profit figures are improving.
4 Many German companies are investing in Turkey.

61
1 You're planning new outlets in Boston and Miami, is that right?
2 They're setting up a subsidiary in Brazil.
3 What are they doing research into?
4 Our competitors are expanding abroad.
5 What are we trying to achieve?
6 Where are you looking for new offices?

62
1 We aren't looking for new markets.
2 They aren't competing for that contract.
3 Our turnover isn't increasing.
4 She isn't working tomorrow.

63
1 They aren't investing in Indonesia.
2 She isn't planning to start a new business.
3 We aren't attracting a lot of new customers.
4 It isn't growing very fast.
5 They aren't launching it until September.

64
1 Man: We're looking for new offices.
  Woman: What's wrong with this building? Too small?
  Man: Well, it's big enough, but it's much too expensive.
2 Woman: So, what do you think of February's sales figures, Fred?
  Man: They're certainly much better than last month's.
  Woman: A lot! And they're still going up, you know.
3 Man: Everybody says Tom and Chris are in Azerbaijan to set up a subsidiary.
  Woman: That's not quite right. Only Chris is there and she just wants to negotiate a contract.
  Man: Oh dear. Sometimes people don't know what they're talking about!
4 Woman: First, I'm going to talk about the features of the new product.
  Man: How about starting with the background to the launch?
  Woman: That's a good idea. Then I can present the features just before the marketing plan.
5 Man: Our marketing strategy isn't good. Sales figures are getting worse.
  Woman: Yes they are, but I think our strategy's fine. In my opinion, there's a problem with our product.
  Man: You mean, it's not right for that market?

65
video; win
value; way

66
1 Their website is very exciting.
2 In my view, it's a waste of money.
3 Which site do you visit most often?
4 The World Wide Web is of great value to advertisers.
5 If you want to visit that site, you need a valid password.
6 I received a virus warning.

67
1 We'll take the early flight.
2 They work hard.
3 I'll do it for them.
4 You'll have to download it.
5 They buy the same software.
6 We'll try all the search engines.

68
1 I'll show you.
2 You'll need it.
3 He'll want one.
4 She'll buy them.
5 We'll watch it.
6 They'll do it.

69
1 A: So the flight's boarding at gate thirty.
  B: No, it's gate thir<u>teen</u> we want.
2 A: Right. So I can come any Tuesday.
  B: Sorry, no. I said any <u>Thursday</u>.

70
1 A: ... and you said check-in is at nine o'clock.
  B: No, it's <u>eight</u> o'clock, I'm afraid.
2 A: ... so that's Janet G-R-A-Y.
  B: Sorry, no. G-R-<u>E</u>-Y. Mrs Janet Grey.
3 A: Excuse me. Is the presentation on the first floor?
  B: No, it's on the <u>third</u> floor. You'd better take the lift!
4 A: ... and your e-mail address is Vermeulen@pe.org.
  B: That's not quite right. It's <u>B</u>-E, as in Belgium.
5 A: Let me just read the postcode back to you: CM20 3GE.
  B: No. It's CM20 3<u>J</u>E.
6 A: So the fax number of their Sofia office is 359 2 968 61 58.
  B: ... 61 <u>98</u>.

71
Speaker 1:   Yes, I can do Thursday afternoon.
Speaker 2:   What's a good time for you?
Speaker 3:   OK. Tomorrow at 9 o'clock is fine for me, too.
Speaker 4:   I'm terribly sorry I didn't come to your presentation. I was ill.
Speaker 5:   If Monday's too busy, maybe Wednesday, then?
Speaker 6:   Sorry, I can't do Monday morning.
Speaker 7:   I'm sorry I didn't make it on time.
Speaker 8:   I'm afraid I can't make Thursday or Friday.
Speaker 9:   How about Tuesday morning instead?
Speaker 10: What day suits you?

72
1 Man: About the contract. Can we discuss it on Tuesday? Monday's no good.
  Woman: You'll be in Stockholm all day Tuesday, so I suggest the day after, if that's convenient.
  Man: Oh, of course. OK then. Fine.
2 Woman: I'm terribly sorry I forgot there was a staff meeting this morning.
  Man: Don't worry. We just discussed things, but we didn't take any decisions.
  Woman: What a pity! Well, I didn't miss much, it seems.
3 Man: So my flight is tomorrow at 2.45.
  Woman: How will you get to the airport? Will you go by metro or do you need a taxi?
  Man: I'll just take the company car this time. I'm coming back early on Wednesday.

4 Woman: Sandra isn't available right now. Would you like to leave a message?
  Man: Yes please. Can she call me back before 11.30?
  Woman: Sure. I'll tell her as soon as she comes out of the meeting.
5 Man: Sorry I didn't make it on time. Our airport is really terrible!
  Woman: What happened? All flights delayed again because of the weather?
  Man: No, no problem with the weather today, but we waited over half an hour for our luggage.
6 Woman: The conference is from 10 o'clock til 4 o'clock, so I could meet you there before or afterwards.
  Man: Let's meet before, say, 9 o'clock at the registration desk? Or in the cafeteria maybe?
  Woman: All right. Let's try their famous espresso as soon as we get there!

73
1 first; requests; hosts
2 staff; store; strategy
3 speak; space; special
4 starts; stopped; strict
5 sports; spirits; specialists

74
1 In Finland, you should never arrive late for an appointment.
2 In many countries, you shouldn't write on business cards.
3 You shouldn't offer your hand to shake immediately.
4 In Germany, you should use the person's title before the surname.
5 In most countries, you shouldn't point your finger at the person you're talking to.
6 So, before you go to a new country, you should do your homework!

75
1 cust<u>om</u>; <u>off</u>er; silence
2 <u>a</u>broad; <u>a</u>dapt; arrive
3 cultur<u>al</u>; document; popul<u>ar</u>
4 appointm<u>e</u>nt; <u>a</u>rrangem<u>e</u>nt; import<u>a</u>nt

76
1 Could I use your phone?
2 Could I use your computer?
3 Would you like a drink?
4 Would you like a sandwich?
5 Could you tell me the way?
6 Could you check these figures?

77
1 Would you like some coffee?
2 Could you spell that for me?
3 Could I use the meeting room?
4 Would you like a copy of the brochure?
5 Could you make the travel arrangements for me?
6 Could I borrow your dictionary?

78
A: So you're saying there are problems in Sales. What kind of problems?
B: Well, it's the representatives. They're complaining about our new work schedule.
A: Do you know what the best thing to do is? Explain to them *why* we changed the schedule.

B: I think they understand the reasons. But, unfortunately, they still don't agree with a lot of the changes.

A: Well, maybe you should talk to them one by one. Try to find out exactly what each one of them is unhappy about.

B: OK then. I'll try that.

79
1 Is it a good idea to call staff by their first names?
2 What's the problem with Paolo? He's always late and he never comes to meetings.
3 Should I accept a business card with my right hand?
4 So, what are normal working hours in your country?
5 I'd like to find out a few things about the history of Brazil.
6 Do people usually drink tea or coffee?

80
work; worked
end; ended
finish; finished
create; created
advertise; advertised
motivate; motivated

81
1 plan; planned
2 wait; waited
3 cope; coped
4 train; trained
5 manage; managed
6 decide; decided
7 invite; invited
8 reward; rewarded
9 organise; organised
10 interrupt; interrupted
11 develop; developed
12 recommend; recommended

82
not; nought
spot; sport
top job; short course

83
1 How often do you write reports?
2 What sorts of bosses have you had?
3 Our office staff don't wear uniforms.
4 Robert has taught abroad for four years.

84
1 She's gained a lot of experience.
2 I've finished everything.
3 He hasn't sent his CV.
4 They've invited her for an interview.
5 We haven't selected anyone yet.
6 We've interviewed everyone.

85
1 Have you learnt anything from your last job?
2 Why are you applying for this job?
3 What didn't you like about your last job?
4 What are your strengths?
5 What do you think of teamwork?
6 Can we contact your referees?

Pearson Education Limited

Edinburgh Gate, Harlow
Essex, CM20 2JE, England
and Associated Companies throughout the world

www.market-leader.net

© Pearson Education Limited 2012

First published 2004
Third edition 2012
ISBN: 978 1 4082 3706 9
Reprinted 2013
Set in: MetaPlus 9.5/13.5
Printed in Slovakia by Neografia
Project Managed by Chris Hartley

All images © Pearson Education